# LON-DONE!
## RUNNING THE GREATER LONDON PARKRUNS

Dean Carter

Copyright 2018 Dean Carter

**Dedicated to:**
Annabelle Madeline Carter

First published 2018 by Dean Carter
copyright Dean Carter
All rights reserved


Also by the same author:

HIKING DIARIES:
End to End: An Adventure on the Pennine Way
Coast to Coast: Walking Wainwright's Way
The Highs and Lows: On the West Highland and Great Glen Way
The Yorkshire Three Peaks EXPERIENCE
The South Downs Way EXPERIENCE
The Capital Ring EXPERIENCE
The London Loop EXPERIENCE

FICTION:
The Hand of the Devil
Hunting Season
Blood Water
The Hammer
Chime the Hour
Four and Twenty
Werewolves of London


This book is not published in association with, or endorsed by parkrun Global

What is Parkrun? **7**

Lon-done **9**

1. Walthamstow **12**

2. Finsbury Park **15**

3. Ally Pally **19**

4. Mile End **22**

5. Northala Fields **25**

6. Tooting Common **29**

7. Southwark **32**

8. Bexley **35**

9. Barking **39**

10. Fulham Palace **43**

11. Riddlesdown **47**

12. Old Deer Park **51**

13. Pymmes **53**

14. Canons Park **56**

15. Valentines Park **59**

16. Osterley Park **62**

17. Hilly Fields **65**

18. Harrow **68**

19. Crystal Palace **71**

20. Beckenham Place Park **74**

21. Beckton **77**

22. Richmond **80**

23. Crane Park **83**

24. Wormwood Scrubs **86**

25. Brockwell Park **89**

26. Dulwich **93**

27. Bedfont Lakes **96**

28. Hackney Marshes **99**

29. Highbury Fields **102**

30. Hampstead Heath **105**

31. Kingston **108**

32. Oak Hill **111**

33. Wanstead Flats **114**

34. Harrow Lodge **117**

35. Roundshaw Downs **120**

36. Orpington **123**

37. Burgess Park **126**

38. Raphael Park **129**

39. Lloyd Park **132**

40. Gunnersbury Park **135**

41. Bromley **138**

42. Greenwich **141**

43. Peckham Rye **144**

44. Grovelands **147**

45. Gladstone **150**

46. Wimbledon **153**

47. Bushy Park **156**

48. Hoblingwell **160**

49. South Norwood **163**

Afterword **166**

Personal Parkrun Picks **167**

Useful Greater London parkrun Information for Tourists **168**

# Introduction

## What is Parkrun?

On Saturday 2nd October 2004 in Bushy Park, Richmond, thirteen runners set off on a five kilometre run through the park, organised by parkrun pioneer Paul Sinton-Hewitt. On that day, parkrun was born. From that one location and thirteen runners, parkrun has expanded to 446 locations in ten different countries and over 1,240,000 runners. It is a modern fitness phenomenon.

So how does parkrun work? It's simple. Once you've registered at www.parkrun.org.uk you are given your own barcode which you can print out and take with you to each event (don't forget it!) When you arrive on Saturday morning (nearly all runs begin at 9am) at your local park, there is a run briefing including information on the course and any safety matters, as well as a mention for any runners reaching key milestones, like their one hundredth run. When you run through the finish funnel five kilometres later you are given a token with another barcode on it. A volunteer with a scanning device will then scan your personal barcode along with the token in order to record your run time. This time is then listed on the results page the same day for you to check your performance against your previous times. This is all completely free, by the way. Parkrun exists because of excellent support from volunteers, local councils and sponsorship deals with companies who are as passionate about the ethos behind parkrun as the parkrun organisers themselves. If you've been thinking of getting involved in the whole 'Couch to 5k' programme, then parkrun should prove invaluable. Once you're confident enough to run with others, you'll find the positive spirit, support and general sense of fun a powerful contributor to achieving your goal. Don't forget – you won't be the only beginner, and you can't come last because one of the volunteers each week is chosen to be the 'tail runner.'

It's not a race. That's very important to remember. In fact the word 'race' is shunned at parkrun, with the less daunting 'time trial' or 'run' being preferable. You should only be competing against yourself, and only then if you want to. I once referred to the Run Director at one event as the Race Director in my blog on tumlbr, and was very politely corrected. Because that's the point of parkrun – you just turn up and run with other likeminded folk. There's no expectation, no cut-off times, no awards for coming first. You tackle that 5k however you like, then you get your barcode scanned and that's it, time to head home or to a nearby café for a coffee and a post-run chat with your fellow runners. Runners' ages range from 4 (under 11s must be accompanied, but can also take part in separate 'Junior parkrun' events) to 80+. Finishing times can range from below 15 minutes for elite runners to over 50 minutes for those taking their time, with the bulk of runners finishing around the half hour mark. Should you feel smug after completing your parkrun? Yes, of course you should. But don't let it show – try to be modest.

Along with corporate sponsorship, volunteers are the lifeblood of parkrun. The number of volunteers varies from week to week and parkrun to parkrun, but the roles include Run Director (responsible for managing the event and giving the pre-run briefing), the route marshals who help ensure runners follow the course correctly and that any hazards are avoided, and the barcode scanners who scan your personal barcode and your finishing token. I volunteered while I was nursing a thigh injury and found it as enjoyable as running (the volunteering, not the injury). In fact many people volunteer having never taken part in the run itself, so it's clearly as rewarding and addictive. You even receive free t-shirts for volunteering milestones like you do for running.

Maybe there are better things to do on a Saturday morning. Sleeping comes to mind. But for me there is something satisfying, enriching and morale-boosting about running five kilometres with a large group of local, similarly-minded folk, all of whom are there to not only get fit but to socialise and encourage each other. They might all be complete strangers, but it doesn't matter, they're there for the same reason as you. It's a feel-good congregation where you feel part of something unique, something special. While there are benefits to solo running like the 'me time,' the 'getting away from it all,' and being able to dictate the speed and length of your run, group running also has its perks. It's believed that running with others leads to improved motivation and performance. It seems we get more out of ourselves while 'running with the pack.'

The other great thing about the Saturday morning run? Sitting down to a breakfast of coffee and croissants knowing that you've already burned off the calories. Like I said - you're allowed to feel smug.

# Lon-done

In 2011 I was staying with my brother in Hampton, when he recommended that we go along to the parkrun in nearby Bushy Park. It was only five kilometres (just over three miles in old money) so I was fine with that, but I'd never heard of the event before, even though it was already seven years old. He told me I would need to register on the parkrun website and print off a barcode that I would need to have scanned at the end of the run in order to register my time. Ok. But how much did it cost to enter? Nothing as it turned out, which seemed really odd to me at the time. When we got to the start area at Bushy Park, the thing that surprised me most was how many people were there. And more were arriving all the time so that by 9am there were several hundred. This happened every week? I couldn't believe it. And the numbers haven't exactly dwindled at Bushy Park since then, despite some runners migrating to nearby events like Richmond Park and Kingston where the numbers are smaller.

I had run Bushy Park and Gunnersbury Park (my local) three times each when in June 2016 I had the crazy idea of visiting all the Greater London parkruns. I thought it would be a great personal challenge and a way to get out and see the capital and some of the many green spaces (London is 50% green after all). Then I discovered there were 45 of them (now 51 at the time of writing). Ah. This could take some time then. If I ran a different one every week I should be done by Summer 2017. I set up a twitter account under the guise of 'Captain Badfoot' (I did actually have a bad foot, having incurred a chronic sprain in early 2014 which still complains now and then) and randomly selected Walthamstow as the first run.

It was a fairly grey, but mild, morning (actually pretty good conditions for running) as I headed off to the Peter May Sports Centre in Walthamstow on Saturday 11th June. The course is three laps around the playing fields and tennis courts with a slight hill to make it interesting, and a nice view across North London. I finished in 23rd place out of a field of 91 runners. Not bad. My time was 24 minutes 41 seconds. Again, not bad at all, but I've since got this down to 21 minutes 57 seconds, the 22 minute barrier being something I had been keen to break for some time. The number of parkruns rose since I started the challenge, making a true sense of completion always out of reach, but so long as I completed the 45 that were in existence when I began my challenge, I would be satisfied. As it turns out, I have completed an additional four as I write this, and although there are more still, I have decided this is enough for now. The highlights have been Alexandra Palace – a fantastic, varied course with an amazing view of the city, Southwark Park – a very friendly parkrun with a flat but interesting course and Beckenham Place Park – partly because this was its inaugural event, and also because it feels like you're genuinely out in the countryside. As I said, my local parkrun is Gunnersbury Park in Ealing which I had to pretty much abandon for over a year. But I was able to run my 50th parkrun there to earn my free, red Tribesports t-shirt. The final parkrun of the challenge was always going to be Bushy Park, so I could end where parkrun began. And what a bittersweet end it was. But even though this was the last one I had planned, I still ran an additional two, at Hoblingwell and South Norwood, and blogged about them. Since that first run at Walthamstow I took my GoPro camera to each event and filmed each run, with difficulty on some occasions, particularly at Dulwich Park in early 2017 when the temperature was -2 degrees and my hands were freezing and almost unresponsive. But it means I can relive each event and research a particular course if I plan on returning. I wrote about each one on my tumblr blog in the hope of inspiring others to join in the phenomenon known as 'parkrun tourism.' Parkrun is great, but parkrun tourism is better – a different park, route and crowd each week. It makes it harder to get that ever elusive personal best time, but that's not the point, remember?

Even if you only give parkrun a go once, you'll be glad you tried it out. It's free. Just don't forget your barcode, don't take the finishing token home with you, and remember . . . It's not a race.

This book is chiefly a chronicle of my London parkrun adventure, but is also meant to be used as a research tool for anyone else thinking of taking on this mammoth task. Hopefully you will be more prepared than I was after reading this, and will have a good sense of what to expect from a particular run, or all of them. With the route descriptions I would recommend having the route map on the relevant parkrun webpage open in from of you so you can see what I'm talking about. It's also a good idea to check out youtube for videos of the individual parkruns. I've posted a good few myself which you should be able to find just by searching for 'dean carter,' 'parkrun,' and the name of the parkrun in question. At the end of this book is a quick summary of my favourite Greater London parkruns, followed by a table of usual stats and a guide to nearest rail stations and toilet facilities (where available). I would also recommend checking out the 'news' section of the event you're planning to visit on parkrun.org.uk before the day of the run, just to be sure there are no cancellations. Facebook and Twitter are also useful places to get up-to-date info on the various parkruns.

Before you embark on your Lon-done journey, just bear in mind the commitment involved. This is no casual parkrun tourism, at least not if you want to complete the whole challenge within a year. This is a parkrun every week for (at the time of writing) 49 weeks. That's almost a year, and you need to factor in illness, injury and any commitments you can't get out of. There may well be moments when you wonder why you are doing it, what you're really getting out of it, but there will be other times when you find yourself, on a Monday morning, already thinking about the next venue, how you're going to get there, what time you need to wake up, how much time you need to allow yourself to be sure you don't get there too late. Thankfully I never turned up to a parkrun too late, but there were some close calls. Early on when I still had a lot of parkruns to choose from, I was able to have backup options. When I first set out to run Ally Pally, I found myself running late and didn't think I would get there in time, so detoured to Finsbury Park instead. Keep in mind what options you may have if you can't make your selected parkrun. You'll have to wait a whole week if you get it wrong, and you'll add a week to your total challenge time. Time is the most frustrating thing about this challenge. You can't complete multiple parkruns in a day (outside of rare, specially planned events), you can't even complete more than one in a week, and this can sometimes be frustrating. There have been times when I've wished I could do one a day. Even now that I've finished the challenge I wish I could do a couple in a weekend. One a week can seem mean when you're a tourist, but until science can give us a way to be in more than one place at once, we'll just have to live with it.

However you want to tackle your own Lon-done challenge, remember that like any hobby or exercise you take up, it has to be fun, otherwise you should just stop and use your time more profitably, doing something you really do enjoy. If you're struggling to get up early on Saturday morning to journey across London, ask yourself if the reluctance is only down to how tired you are, and not down to a lack of enthusiasm or because you no longer believe in what you are doing. However, sometimes, if you find yourself doubting what you're doing, it's best to just lace up your shoes and go anyway. Visiting somewhere new, meeting new people and running a new course is hardly a waste of a Saturday morning.

# 1. Walthamstow
11th June, 2016
'The tourist'


Preamble

'Tourist' is the official Parkrun term for a runner visiting a parkrun other than their local. It's what I now am. I'm standing in a small huddle of eager newcomers listening to a pre-run briefing. I'm the only 'tourist' in the huddle, the others are locals who have come along to run for the first time. The run director asks me where I'm from and I tell her Ealing. This elicits a respectful 'wow' and a smile, though she then goes on to diminish its impact by telling us that someone came over from Holland to do the parkrun not long ago. Wow. She also tells the group that parkrunning can become an addiction. Some of the runners milling around us are sporting their '50' or '100' t-shirts, denoting the milestones of 50 and 100 parkruns completed. I am among fanatics. Correction – I am a fanatic among fanatics, that is if I stick to my plan and actually complete all 45 (at the time of writing) Greater London parkruns. Part of me wishes the runs took place more regularly than every Saturday so I could complete the challenge quicker, while another part of me wishes I'd never got the crazy idea in my head in the first place.

Backtracking a little, I left home in West Ealing at just after 7am in order to get to the Peter May Sports Centre in Walthamstow in good time. I caught a train from West Ealing to Paddington, changing to the Circle Line to get to Liverpool Street and then up to Highams Park station on an overland train. In all, the journey took me about an hour and twenty minutes. Not as bad as I had thought, and no hold ups. I walked and jogged a little to the sports centre (having previously used Google Maps to check the route there from the station), used the changing room and toilet and limbered up a bit outside before being called over to the huddle.

The run director explained the route to us newbies. I'd already checked it out via the Walthamstow parkrun homepage at http://www.parkrun.org.uk/walthamstow/course/ and saw that it was three laps of the playing fields. I quite liked this idea as it meant once you'd completed the first lap you then knew exactly what to expect for the next two and could pace yourself accordingly. Once we were briefed there were a few minutes for a further warm up before everyone was called together for the general run briefing. Again the course was explained, as well as the procedure for getting your bar code scanned at the finish line (this is how your time for the run is recorded, with the results being posted online in the next day or so). There had been problems previously with scanning the bar codes, but they had been given a new scanner which they seemed pretty thrilled about. There were probably less than a hundred people assembled, a stark contrast to the Bushy Park parkrun that I'd taken part in a few times. That normally attracted several hundred, and was the very first organised parkrun, and the first parkrun I'd experienced. I decided it might be apt to save that parkrun for last, finishing my challenge where it all started for me. At Walthamstow, as at all parkruns, I'm sure, there was a good mix of runners from all age groups and abilities.

The briefing over, it was then just a matter of waiting for the countdown. I filmed the huddle with my new GoPro camera, or at least believed I did. It was only while reviewing the footage at home the next day that I realised I'd been filming when I thought I wasn't, and vice versa. Lots of upside down shots of my legs and the inside of my backpack. Oh well.


The Course

There was a shout of encouragement and the group lurched forward. I started my fitbit watch and music player and started running. From the start the route heads down toward the road to the centre, with the centre on your right, then turns left by a big tree where I had left my backpack and toward the finish line funnel. I had no intention of running fast at the beginning so I relaxed into the run to begin with and just got the lie of the course which soon turns left and heads uphill, the only uphill section of the course and a stretch that, thankfully, doesn't outstay its welcome. At the top the course turns left, still uphill for a short section before evening out. Already there was a gap forming with the leaders breaking away, but the bulk of the runners were behind me, and I now started to speed up and set a more challenging pace for myself. At the end of the straight the course turns left and goes downhill slightly, before mounting an unexpected but not challenging hump at the end, leading to a smaller field, and then following the fence around the car park and tennis courts. The run director had told us that a tree had fallen near the start line and the route had been changed slightly to avoid it. I was expecting it after passing the tennis courts, but couldn't see any sign of a fallen tree, so when I turned the corner I nearly ran into the tape cordoning the area off. I corrected my mistake and ran on through the start line and into lap two.

I kept the pace and managed to overtake several people on the second lap, finding that although I hadn't slept well the previous two nights I had plenty of energy for it. Into the third lap I was still going strong, though by the time I rounded the tree and headed toward the finish funnel, I only had enough in me for a half-sprint finish. Still, it was enough. I hadn't intended to go all out on the first of my forty-five Greater London parkruns, just getting there on time and completing it was enough.

After getting my bar code scanned I caught my breath, had a drink then headed off. I was worn out, but I'd already planned to get the train to Chingford and walk another stretch of the London Loop (I ended up walking sixteen long miles on legs that felt like jelly to begin with).

The vibe at Walthamstow had been a good one. Everyone was enjoying themselves and encouraging each other. There was no rivalry, just community spirit. I was actually a little gutted to think that I'd probably never take part in the Walthamstow parkrun again, but at the same time I knew that that kind of spirit and positive energy would be there at the next parkrun.

Position: 23 out of 91
Time: 24 minutes, 41 seconds

Walthamstow parkrun was a nice and steady start to my parkrun challenge. I gave myself plenty of time to get to the venue and have a warm up before the run began. I tried not to think of the overall challenge as a long, hard slog that would take me over a year, but more an exciting adventure that would keep me occupied for the next twelve months and beyond.

# 2. Finsbury Park

18th June, 2016
'The backup plan'


Preamble

Oh dear. It's a good thing that parkrun itself is simple, well-organised and well-run (no pun intended) on the day, otherwise I don't think my Lon-Done challenge would ever have worked.
My intention was to do Ally Pally (Alexandra Palace) parkrun this week, firstly because it's a fantastic location, secondly because the course looked really good, and third because, alphabetically, it was at the top of the list of Greater London parkruns. Sadly, although I was up nice and early, I somehow delayed leaving the flat, waited longer than expected for a bus to Ealing Common station, and finding myself with less time than was needed to get to Wood Green station. At least not without a mad, idiotic dash to Alexandra Park. Luckily, Finsbury Park was also on the Piccadilly Line, so although I didn't really want to change my plans, I decided to play it safe and do that parkrun this week instead. Even with this alteration to the plan I was worried I wouldn't make it in time, and while sat reading J.G. Ballard's *High Rise* on my Kindle I found myself checking my watch and looking up each time the train pulled into a station. Luckily I reached Finsbury Park station with twenty or so minutes to spare, so all was good.
After finding my way to the park, which thankfully was fairly straightforward, I made my way (by following the other runners) to the start of the course which is on the wide path near the café. I headed over to a bench, took off my jeans and top, then put my cap on and my headstrap with GoPro camera attached. I've tried running with the GoPro a few times now, and each time I learn something new and get closer to properly filming a run. I thought I'd have it sorted today, and though I was nearly there, I didn't quite get the cigar. I have the GoPro app on my phone, and using this I was able to see the video feed from the camera while it was on my head so I could check that it was level. The level, however, wasn't the problem, the positioning was. It only occurred to me

later that when I had been viewing the video feed on my phone, I was looking down, so everything looked fine. When running I was looking straight ahead, which meant that for most of the run the camera was taking high definition video footage of the tops of trees. Still, after realising my mistake I chalked it up to experience and brought myself one step closer to filming a run properly.

So, with the camera already searching for squirrels in the branches above, I made my way over to the parkrun huddle, and after leaving my bag somewhere safe joined the crowd that was already gathering by the start line. The run organiser soon fired up her megaphone and went through the run briefing, welcoming first-timers and tourists (like myself) before thanking the volunteers. Compared to Walthamstow this was a pretty brief preamble, but it was getting close to 9am, so with the introduction out of the way we were let loose on the two-lap course.

The Course

It was a larger crowd than Walthamstow: 242 runners compared to 91 and although (as is normal) we were quite bunched up at the start, the runners soon spread out and we headed down the first stretch of path, past the tennis courts to the near hairpin bend at the end where we turned left and started to head up the gradual incline along the South-East section of the park. I would never complain about inclines (I think it's misleading to refer to them as 'hills') in parkruns or other runs, as there is something distinctly unsatisfying about a course that's entirely on the flat. It feels almost like cheating. That's not to say I actually like inclines though, even gradual ones like this, so I try to just keep a good speed up and remind myself that it can't last forever. This one does last a fair while though to be honest, but end it does and actually turns downhill just after curving around to the left, passing between rows of trees before reaching a left turn and two cheering marshals. Then it's uphill again. This incline is shorter, but steeper, so getting up a head of steam isn't really an option unless you're a far better athlete than me or are on your second lap and really giving it everything you've got. At the top of the slope the course continues ahead across a couple of paths before leaning left around the small lake, through the middle of a garden area, past the playground and 'Furtherafield' gallery and back toward the path where the run began. It was now time for the second lap. My thoughts now were to keep a good, steady pace and not burn myself out on the uphill sections. I had started my Fitbit watch to record the run, but for some reason (maybe due to problems with GPS coverage) it had my average pace at an unlikely 10.5 minutes per mile and didn't record the distance properly. If I had concentrated on the time rather than distance I'd have realised that the run must end after completing the second lap. But because, as I neared the end of the second lap, the watch was only registering 2.5 miles (instead of the 3.1 for a 5k) I assumed I would have to do another lap, or maybe half a lap. So after circling the lake for a second time and heading toward the start, I was surprised to find myself following the runners in front of me through the finishing funnel. This isn't to suggest that I was feeling great and could have easily run another lap, but I had been expecting it. I took my finishing bar code and wandered about in a bit of a daze looking for a volunteer so I could confirm I'd actually done the whole course. I did this and, on seeing the time on my watch was just over 24 minutes, realised it was indeed the dodgy distance registered on the watch that had caused the confusion, and I should have relied on the timing all along. I found a volunteer to scan the barcode on my wristband and the one I had been given, then found my bag under the nearby tree where the nice volunteer had left it for me.

So, despite technology failing me (the watch), and me failing technology (the GoPro) I had managed to knock off another Greater London parkrun, and it had been another good one. Again the crowd was enthusiastic and encouraging of each other, and the volunteers were many and helpful. I do like Finsbury Park. I've been there a few times now and it does seem to have a little bit of everything. Check it out.

Having completed the Capital Ring trail, and knowing it passed through Finsbury Park, and feeling like I hadn't quite exerted myself as much as I should have, I took off out of the park and followed the Capital Ring for a couple of miles along the Parkland Walk to Highgate Station where I had a fantastic coffee and caught the Northern Line to Tottenham Court Road, then the Central Line back to Ealing.


Position: 82 out of 242
Time: 24 minutes, 7 seconds.

Considering the inclines and not realising where/when the finish was, I'm fairly satisfied with the result. I had hoped that I would be under 24 minutes, but as the course will be changing each week, getting better and better times will be tricky. I actually guessed that my position would be 83 before I found out what it actually was, based on the fact that I'm usually at the back of the first third to finish.

## 3. Ally Pally
25th June, 2016
'Come together'


Preamble

My parkrun challenge was now starting to really come together, if only I could get the filming right (see below). Not wanting to make the same mistake as last week, I made sure I left the house with enough time to get to the venue at Ally Pally. I caught the bus at the bottom of the road to Ealing Common station, then caught a Piccadilly Line train all the way to Wood Green. From there it was a simple case of following Station Road all the way to Alexandra Palace station, then crossing the footbridge to the park on the other side. I had only been to Alexandra Palace once before, last year and it had been a fairly grey day so a bit of a disappointment. But despite recent wet weather today was much nicer, and more than favourable conditions for the parkrun. I found the avenue where I knew the run started and, being half an hour early, wasn't surprised to find there was no one there. I knew that people often turned up at the last minute for parkruns, so I wasn't worried but actually quite happy to have arrived with time to spare.
I ducked into the trees to get changed and put on my GoPro and headstrap. I'd had a lot of 'fun' in the last two weeks trying to work out how to film a run with the camera. It seems simple in concept – just set 'record' on the camera, attach the headstrap to your head and run, but there are a few things that can go wrong. On one training run the camera had been skewed to one side so it looked (when reviewing the footage) that I was running on a slope. Running at Finsbury Park the week before I'd had the camera pointed up too much so that for most of the run I had been filming the treetops rather than anything interesting, so this time I was determined to get it right and film the whole run. Properly. I synced my phone with the GoPro and did a few tests to ensure the camera was aimed in the right direction. Other runners had started to turn up and congregate at the start now, so I grabbed my bag and jogged down to join them. When it was time to form up I joined the crowd, concerned that I'd

positioned myself too far back again and would have to get around a few people before I could break free. It was probably good that I didn't start nearer the front however, as I think I'd have gone too fast out of the gate and worn myself down too early. One problem I'm going to have to live with doing the 45 (at the time of writing) park challenge is being faced with a new course each week and not being able to get to know them well enough. I know the Gunnnersbury Park parkrun course better than any because it's my local one, and in training the week before the Ally Pally run I ran a faster 5k than I had since last year. I'm sure this is because I know the course and know what to expect so I know how to pace myself. Still, I like a challenge and intend to get a 5k PB at some point despite facing a new course each week.

The Course

When the time came we were all let loose and surged along the avenue toward the open section of the park along the track toward the sign pointing to the left. The sun was shining now and it was turning out to be a glorious morning. The runners, like a disbanded conga line, was already spreading out as it curved around and followed the track to the bottom of the grass before turning left along the rough, muddy perimeter track. It got a little tricky here as there were still a lot of runners together, vying for the same thin stretch of path, but everyone was very considerate to each other and prepared to make room. It was great to see folk with dogs running the course too. Up ahead at the corner of the park, everyone turned left and followed the outside of the cricket pitch on a much wider tarmac path, before taking another rough track toward the wooded section of the course. Passing over a small footbridge there came a very muddy, slippery section that required care, before turning left and heading slightly uphill now.
The muddy track gave out onto the avenue not far from the start point, crossing over to a track that soon led quite steeply uphill. It was temping to walk this section, but any kind of stopping felt like giving in, so I pressed on. It isn't a long section anyway. At the top, the track turned left and went downhill slightly to begin with. This is a long straight section, and although you can kind of distract yourself with the views of Alexandra Palace itself when it comes into view to the right, it is easy to feel like this stretch is never going to end. It even starts to go uphill later on, but worse is to come. Although you turn left from here onto a downhill section, it is

a little too steep to enjoy or take advantage of, and needs a controlled descent to avoid pummelling your knees. At the bottom of the slope was another left turn and a short stretch before turning right and starting on the second lap around the grass and the cricket pitch. Although there were less people around me on the second lap, I already felt like I'd used up everything I had, and was unable to maintain a fast pace, so by the time I reached the finish line I'd almost clocked up twenty-five minutes, about two more than I'd have liked. I blame this on spending too much time setting up the camera before the run, and not enough time warming up. There was also the slightly technical nature of the course that I hadn't had a chance to try out before. But never mind, there was still a lot of time to get that PB. What a great course though. I'd love to return and run the Ally Pally parkrun again, and would urge all parkrunners thinking of a little tourism to try it out. Afterwards you can grab a coffee then check out the incredible view of the capital from the top of the hill. Outstanding. All the runners and volunteers were terrific. Onwards and upwards!

Position: 47 out of 158
Time: 24 minutes, 44 seconds.

If I'd spent more time warming up than fiddling with the camera I might have been in better shape to get a faster time than the week before. That said, the course does get technical in a couple of places with some uphill sections and one quite steep downhill that can impact your time. I might even, tentatively, recommend using off-road shoes for this parkrun if the weather has been bad and you're dead set on getting a fast time. I was too far back at the beginning to really let loose, though this might have caused me to run too fast too soon. Great course and location though.

## 4. Mile End
2nd July, 2016
'Out and back'

Preamble

Mile End is the first 'out and back' parkrun course I've run, and it's a really cool one. In fact, you might be forgiven for thinking Mile End Park was designed for parkrunners as the main path used for the run splits into two for a large section, allowing runners to separate out depending on which direction they're heading in. This not only helps give you an idea of where you are in the run, but also gives everyone a chance to shout encouragement to each other.
I was a little worn out before starting this run, as I'd helped my brother move house the day before, possibly one of the most intensive workouts you can have, and had gotten back home at 11.30pm, shattered and ready for bed but with a few minutes to decide which parkrun to do in the morning. I had originally planned to do Kingston as it was near to Hampton where my brother lived (he's actually really close to Bushy Park, but I wanted to save that parkrun until last), but since he'd moved most of his furniture (leaving nothing comfy to sleep on) and it wasn't imperative that I do Kingston at this point, I decided to travel home to Ealing on the Friday night and then choose a different parkrun in the morning. Looking at my list I saw that, alphabetically, Barking was next after Ally Pally, and after checking the travel details via tfl.gov.uk, I decided to head there, with Mile End as a backup in case I couldn't get there in time.
I was up with the alarm and, unsurprisingly, in two minds as to whether to get out of bed. Knowing how disappointed I'd be if I missed the parkrun however, I managed to rise and get myself ready. Even with plenty of time I still left the flat late and knew I'd be pushing my luck with Barking, so decided to go for Mile End instead. I caught a Central Line train and read some more of Debra Bourne's excellent book *Parkrun: Much More than Just a Run in the Park*. When I reached Mile End station I realised I'd been there before during a charity walk for work, and guessed that the run would be along the park by the canal. I didn't know where the start was

though, so I had to get the parkrun website up on my phone to check the course. I jogged in the direction of the running track and soon saw other runners heading there too. When I got to the start point I dropped my bag by one of the benches, took off my long sleeve top and trousers and then went for a quick warm up run with about fifteen minutes to spare before the run started. My legs felt a bit tender after all the work the day before, but I wasn't too fussed about getting a fast time. I'd take it easy if necessary and just enjoy it. Everyone was congregating now, so I grabbed my GoPro camera and joined them. I decided not to use the headstrap for the camera this time and just hold the camera in my hand. I'd tried this technique a few weeks earlier at Walthamstow but had completely messed up the recording, believing I was switching the camera on when I was actually turning it off, and vice versa. This time I got it right and managed to capture some good footage, without it interfering with my run too much.

The Course

After a brief intro and going over of rules from the run director we were off. The course begins to the left (from the runners' point of view) of Mile End Park Stadium with the track splitting into two with trees down the middle. Most runners kept to the right hand path – I'm not sure if they've been instructed to do this in the past or because everyone follows the runners in front, but it made sense, and when I found myself on the left on the second lap I crossed over as soon as I could in case any runners started coming back toward me. The course soon heads up a slight rise and curves around to the left as it dips down again and nears the canal before bearing right again through another garden area before rising over the Green Bridge over Mile End Road and curving down to the left, then right around the Mile End Art Pavilion, and then left again onto the canal, which it follows until it returns to the original path by the small, round hill, completing a loop. It was now time to head back to the start. I felt I was running pretty well and not slowing down due to starting too quickly which I had been doing on previous runs. I had done some interval training during the week which may have helped with this, and my overall attitude today of just taking it easy may also have contributed and prevented me from overdoing it. Once I reached the start it was time to turn around and complete lap two, and I made sure to allow plenty of room for a female runner with her stroller. She was going fast, even with her passenger. For the second lap I decided to keep it comfortable but not allow myself to drop back, and found a couple of runners to use as unwitting pacers. When I returned to the starting area for the second time to finish the run I could actually have sprinted a lot faster a lot earlier, so I clearly had more in the tank than I thought. I grabbed a token and had my barcode and the token scanned. I then remembered to stop my watch, thinking twenty-three minutes, thirty seconds was too fast. As it turned out the time was actually twenty-three minutes twenty one seconds. This was my best time this season and in the parkrun challenge so far.

Position: 77 out of 208
Time: 23 minutes, 21 seconds.

It just goes to show that strenuous exercise the day before a 5k doesn't necessarily mean your performance will suffer. I was fiddling with the camera a bit during the run which slowed me down a bit, and I was quite tentative in general, and not aggressive enough coming up to the finish line, so I think I could have gotten the time under twenty-three minutes. Something to think about for next week. Again, the marshals were outstanding, everyone seemed to have a great time, and the course itself is great. Another one I'd love to do again.

## 5. Northala Fields
9th July, 2016
'Perfect timing'


Preamble

This was a local run, and I could have run to the start from home, but in the end I decided to trust public transport more than my legs. Also, as it was my birthday, I was determined to celebrate by getting a 5k PB, so I wanted to make sure I had plenty of energy. It had been a tiring week. I'd had a cold, been hungover, and not slept as much as I should. Friday night in particular was awful as I didn't get to sleep until 4am, having set the alarm for Saturday morning at 7.15am. But I wasn't going to miss the run so, bleary-eyed, I hauled myself out of bed, had breakfast and got dressed, now sporting my Captain Badfoot (twitter name) t-shirt with the locations and dates of the parkruns I'd completed so far (scrawled on the back in permanent marker). Well, since there are no medals or badges I had to do something . . .

I left the flat and walked around the corner to catch an E7 bus to the bottom of Rectory Park. The journey only took around twenty minutes, a lot shorter than I'd expected, so I had plenty of time to walk across the park, find the start point and do some warming up. I had been indecisive about whether to wear my GoPro in the headstrap like I'd done at Ally Pally, or carry it in my hand and film like I'd done the week before at Mile End. In the end the weather (overcast but dry) made the decision for me – it was only worth using the headstrap, I thought, if the weather was good. I reached the hills next to the A40 and found a small group of volunteers and runners already assembled. The four large mounds at Northala Fields were constructed using rubble from the demolition of the original Wembley stadium. I'd run around this area a few times before when I'd lived in Greenford, and the view from the top of the highest hill is pretty impressive. I warmed up a bit by jogging around the hills and the fishing lakes, watching the group of people near the start grow bigger and bigger. In fact the numbers had swelled dramatically (as they tend to do with parkruns) by ten minutes to nine, when the run director gave his pre-run briefing. He asked if there were any parkrun tourists so I put my hand up. Another tourist there was from Mile End which, coincidentally, was the parkrun I went to last week. The run director also asked if anyone was celebrating any milestones like birthdays etc., but I'd already had enough of the limelight so I kept my mouth shut.

After the entertaining introduction it was time to move away from the gathering area near the café and walk down the path to the start point. I must have been preoccupied with the GoPro and/or the ipod, as when I looked up to check if the crowd had started moving I realised I was right at the back. I seemed to do this every week, which made chasing a PB all the more harder by having to get around people at the start. But it is a run, not a race after all, so I wasn't annoyed, I'd just have to make the time up later on the course. Then came the sound of the whistle, and the inevitable surge forward.

The Course

We started running back in the direction of the café, to the right of the hills, then took a sharp left to run around the side, then the back of the hills, before running down the slight downhill path between them, back through the main gathering area and down between the fishing lakes through the narrower green area by the side of the golf course and on to Rectory Park. On reaching the park the course takes a sharp right then left turn onto a tree-covered path for a short stretch before opening out onto the field and heading toward the main road. I didn't realise the course went onto the pavement then followed the outside of the park before heading back in and along its East side. I could only see several runners on the path ahead of me and not along the far side of the field (because they were on the pavement on the other side of the trees) so I was duped into thinking I wasn't far behind the leaders. As if. But the fantasy didn't last long. Once on the pavement I realised what was actually going on and came back down to Earth. At this point, from checking my watch, I knew I was keeping a reasonable 7 – 7.5 minutes a mile pace, and so had a chance of getting a personal best time. All I needed to do was not slow down too much but also not speed up and wear myself out. The field was nice and spread out with most runners behind me, and I didn't feel any pressure just yet. If I kept it together I could do it.

We left Rectory Park once more and headed back toward the lakes and hills. Passing by the café again one of the volunteers was ringing a bell merrily every time someone passed. We headed up the slight rise and this time ran behind the hills in the opposite direction to return to the path we began on with a sharp right turn. I knew the finish was ahead on this straight now, but not exactly where. Was it by the café or was it further on by the start line? Surely not, otherwise runners from two different directions would be hurtling into each other. It had to be by the café.

My personal best for the 5k distance up to this point was 22.59 which I achieved last summer in Gunnersbury Park, my home parkrun. This time was now rapidly approaching. I dug in and sped up as much as I could, feeling my lungs heaving, and hearing myself pant even over the music in my ears. 22.50 turned into 22.51, then 22.52, 22.53 . . . On and on. I could see runners standing around up ahead. That had to be the finish. God, please! 22.54, 22.55, 22.56 . . .

I stopped looking at my watch and just plunged for the finish. I took my finish token from the volunteer then wandered around in a bit of a daze, looking for someone to scan my barcode and token. I joined the queue. The volunteer was having a bit of trouble getting the scanner to recognize a barcode, but after giving the sensor a bit of a clean it was working again. I had the barcode on my wristband scanned, then handed him my token and that was that. I had a feeling I had either equalled my personal best or beaten it by a second or two, but it was impossible to be sure as I'd stopped my watch too late.

I left Northala Fields in a rush because I had to get back home to shower then leave to catch a train to Paddington and then on to Worcester and Tenbury Wells to visit my parents. But despite how much I was rushed, and despite the tight schedule it was impossible not to appreciate, yet again, the best part of Parkrun - running with others, with the pack. Running on my own is great, but when it comes to parkrun day, running with others, even if, as is often the case with parkrun tourism they are all complete strangers, it is so much more fulfilling, more engaging to be part of a group.


Position: 43 out of 223
Time: 22 minutes, 57 seconds (PB).*

As I've said before - it's difficult to gauge improvement accurately when running a different course every week, but my fitness certainly feels like it has improved over the past few weeks. I was really hoping to get below 23 minutes and beat my PB of 22.59, and I did it. Only by two seconds but this is how it works. PBs are very rarely 'smashed' just ever so slightly nudged aside. The next target will be getting below 22.30. Achievable, but I need to improve my approach – getting nearer to the front of the pack when the run starts and doing more interval training to get my average pace down. Oh and the foot . . . My weak right foot that has been injured more times than I can count and still hasn't recovered fully from a chronic sprain over two years ago, is still a worry. While the pain has been more down than up the last few weeks, there is still a possibility that the injury will flare up again and cause me problems. That said, the 'foot' is going to have to get incredibly 'bad' to make me give up on my 45 Parks quest. I'm just loving it way too much.

*On checking my stats a week later I realised it wasn't a PB after all! My previous best time for the 5k (at Gunnersbury) was 22.56, so I missed it by a second. However . . .

# 6. Tooting Common
16th July, 2016
'Triangle'


Preamble

I only realised a few days ago that I was signed up to a 10k race in Regents Park this Sunday, which came as a surprise as I was sure it was in August. Still, it didn't really make much difference as I wasn't going to be trying for a 10k PB, I just wanted to see how I did at that distance having not run one for a while. So Tooting was not only another parkrun crossed off the list, but also a nice warm up for the race the day after.
I was up at 6.15am and out of the house by 7.10, jogging a little on the way to Ealing Broadway station to get the legs warmed up. They were aching a little from a long hike a couple of days before, but they felt like there was plenty left in them for the 5k and 10k the next day, provided I didn't go mad trying to get a PB two weeks in a row. I caught a Central Line train to Oxford Circus, then the Victoria Line to Stockwell where I changed to the Northern Line to get to Tooting Bec station. The sky was overcast but warm, and again (wary of tempting fate) I wondered at how it never seemed to rain on a parkrun. I mean, it must have done . . . at some point . . . surely?
Not knowing the area (something I was used to now as a parkrun tourist), I had to get my phone out and check the map to find my way to the common, which was only a short walk down Tooting Bec Road. I had crossed the common twice before while walking the Capital Ring, but it had been in the middle of a day's hike so I had no idea where the tube stations were.
When I reached the common I jogged in the direction of the café which I thought was where the run started. I saw a small group of people setting up what looked suspiciously like a finishing funnel on the path toward the café, and after checking the course map further on I realised that was where the parkrun started. At the café I stopped and circled the building hoping to find a loo, but didn't have any luck. I was thinking of checking the map on my phone again but couldn't be bothered to get it out of my rucksack, so instead ran down the path (part of the parkrun course)

looking for likely buildings that may house a convenience. I couldn't find anything by the playground or tennis courts, but when I reached the car park I found a toilet block nearby. Unfortunately the Gents was locked, so after crossing the road to look for a loo near the stadium, and giving up, I retraced my steps back on to the common as the time for the run was drawing near. There's probably a good reason why the toilets are locked and gathering cobwebs, but this is no consolation when you really need to go. I realised I'd just have to cross my legs, which should make the run interesting. As it turned out, the toilets were in the café, so I must have somehow missed them.

When I arrived back at the start of the run I found a large group had already gathered and was growing by the second. After taking my GoPro camera from my bag and having a drink I left the bag at the drop point and wandered around for a bit, eavesdropping on the briefing for new runners, then gathering with everyone for the main run briefing which, as usual for parkrun, was brief but informative and entertaining. It was interesting to hear that the Tooting parkrun was still in its trial period, and although it should have received a decision on whether it was going to be allowed to continue, might actually just be getting its trial period extended. I hope the council gives its consent, there were lot of very keen and appreciative runners there with me who would no doubt be gutted if it couldn't continue.


The Course

It was time to form up at the start point and this time I was sure to get closer to the front, but not too close as I almost ended up with the runners who were going for a nineteen minute time. Not quite ready for that yet . . . We were given a quick 'three, two, one' and then were off, heading down a short stretch to turn right and start the first lap of a triangular course. I was able to soon relax (if that's the right word) into a nice pace and enjoy the new course, filming every now and again when the course changed direction. At the end of the first stretch the course turned left to follow Tooting Bec Road for the shortest side of the triangle before turning left on a path leading back into the common, passing to the right of the pond at one point and eventually coming to the northernmost point of the course, near the café to then begin the second lap. I was a bit worried about overdoing it here but thankfully was able to more or less maintain my starting pace and not slow down. For this and the third (and final) lap I was more or less keeping pace with a female runner and her buggy, containing a very excited and vocal young man who clearly wouldn't have wanted to be anywhere else. I tried to imagine what it would be like if I had been pushed around a course by one or both of my parents when I had been his age. Must be so much fun. Hope it inspires him to run when he's older.

After completing lap three it was time to turn off the odd-shaped, triangular course and head back down the short straight and onto the grass toward the finish funnel. In front of me was a chap wearing a t-shirt that said 'go all out' on the back. Sorry, but even in the closing metres I didn't have enough energy left to sprint. I need to work on that. I did the obligatory puffing and panting, then looked around for a volunteer with a scanner. Checking my watch afterwards, it read 23.08, although I'd stopped it late. I wondered how close I'd come to my 5k PB of 22.56. It was only while writing this that I realised I hadn't in fact beaten my PB on my birthday the week before as I had thought, but missed it by one second. I wonder . . .

Position: 90 out of 365
Time: 22 minutes, 52 seconds (PB).*

It was great to find that although I hadn't PB'd the week before, I had done it this week. I didn't set out to get a best time, but I didn't slack off during the run either, and although there were several turns, there were no inclines to speak of, so it made good conditions for getting a PB. I'm encouraged to keep trying to improve and bring the time down. Tooting is another great parkrun course and I have no doubt that a lot of runners have PB'd several times there. I hope they get the go ahead to make it a permanent fixture on the common. 365 runners is not a small number and indicates how popular the event is already.

*Double-checked it this time.

# 7. Southwark
23rd July, 2016
'We have cake'


Preamble

It's a bit of a coincidence that I've become interested in collecting vinyl records, as I'm beginning to sound like a broken one, i.e. this was another fantastic parkrun with a great location, great course and a great vibe. Like all the other parkruns I've completed so far, I could happily return to Southwark every week to run. I loved it.
To paraphrase my favourite film *Withnail and I*, I ran the Southwark parkrun by mistake. Using the random number generator app on my phone earlier in the week I had selected Bexley as this week's parkrun, and had made sure I was up early enough (6 o'clock) to get organised and out of the house in time to catch the 6.58am District Line train from Ealing Broadway to Victoria. The train was delayed a couple of times on the way (presumably to 'even out gaps in the service'), but on reaching Victoria I still had a couple of minutes to get to the train so I double-timed it. Sadly, when I reached the first platform and asked the nearby guard which train would take me to Welling (one of the nearest stations to Bexley), he nodded over his shoulder.
'That one.'
'What, the one pulling away right now?' I asked.
'Yep,' he replied, looking and sounding like he was about to fall asleep right there and then. Great. I sighed and tramped off back to the underground, already deciding that rather than waste time trying to find another station where I could catch an overland train to Welling, I would just play it safe and revert to the backup plan of going to London Bridge, then running along the road to Southwark Park. It was a good thing I checked the map for Southwark as well as Bexley earlier in the week. You would think that Southwark station would be the nearest one to the park, but it isn't. Bermondsey is actually the best bet, although I didn't realise this until I'd already got off at London Bridge and ran half a mile or so

down the road. Still, it was fine, I would go via Bermondsey on the way home, and besides, I still had plenty of time before the run started.

On entering Southwark Park I had a quick look at the board to compare it to the parkrun course map on my phone so I could head in the direction of the start of the run, but also to check out where the toilets were. I walked in the direction of the bandstand, then turned left and jogged along an outside path for a while until I came to the café. I must have been early as the owner was still setting up, and after some encouragement he let me in to use the loo. I then realised I only had a quarter of an hour left, so ran off in the general direction of the start to find a group already gathered. I took a few photos of the pre-run huddle as I've gotten used to doing now, and recorded a quick clip with my GoPro camera. I've given up on using the headstrap now, even though I keep telling myself if it's really good weather I'll use it. And it was great weather today, but did the headstrap come out? Nope. I think it's partly because I have to put it on then use my phone to see the video feed and adjust it so it's at the right level, which can be finicky, and partly because even though it's obvious to everyone what I'm doing, I think I still look a bit silly with a camera stuck to my head. Who wouldn't? Besides, I think I've got the knack of running with the camera in my hand now. So long as it doesn't start to affect my run too much and slow me down, it's fine.

There was the usual pre-briefing briefing for newcomers (and there seemed to be a lot of them today, which was great) then the full pre-run briefing with the great news that today was Southwark's 150th parkrun. A fantastic milestone, and an excuse (if there ever needs to be one) for a picnic (including cake) afterwards. There were a couple of runner milestones to mention and a thank you to the volunteers, then a quick countdown and it was time to move.

The Course

I was closer to the front than usual, though again it was good that I wasn't too close as I could have gone too fast too early. As it was I still started strong and had to ease back slightly on the second and third laps to avoid burning out. The group headed forward along the tree-lined path by the finish funnel until, just before the café, we were directed left by a volunteer, to follow the path first around the play area, then right, around the lake, and the down a long, straight path with trees in the middle, looping to the right to double-back on ourselves at the end and head back down the path and around the outside of the park. This switchback section, like the one at Mile End, was great as you could see other runners behind you in the pack now coming towards you. The course started turning left toward the end and went down a small dip then alongside the running track. A guy with long hair and his jacket tied around his waist was running on the grass by the side of the path. He wasn't doing the parkrun, and he seemed overdressed, but who cares? He was running and clearly loving life. Good on him. Further on it was time to turn left and after a fairly short section we passed the start of the run and a small group of very enthusiastic, cheering volunteers, before reaching the point where the course turns left again by the cafe. Lap one was done and so far so good. I knew I'd have to ease back a little on the next two laps, but at the same time I wasn't struggling, so I kept going strong, and on the final turn did my best to sprint to the finish line. To be honest I had enough energy to start my sprint for the line earlier, and noticed several other people do exactly that, but as usual, being a tourist and not knowing the course and its quirks, it was difficult to get this right. Still, I looked at my watch at the end and although I checked it after I'd officially finished, it was still under 23 minutes, which meant I was close to my new PB of 22.52. But how close?

Position: 55 out of 237
Time: 22 minutes, 52 seconds

So I'd actually equalled my PB and was in the first quarter of the group to finish. I was more than happy with the result, and confident that if I had done the same course again a week later I'd beat it. That, however, was not to be as there were plenty more parkruns waiting. I really enjoyed running at Southwark Park. The park itself is gorgeous and well-maintained, the course is well-designed with plenty of scenery, and travel-wise it should be easy for most people in London to get to. The runners were a friendly, lively bunch, and the volunteers were fantastic.

Oh, and they have cake.

Well . . . they did.

# 8. Bexley
30th July, 2016
'Cheers!'


Preamble

This week had been light on sleep mainly, I think, due to a) the fluctuating temperatures, and b) the loud, bizarre arguments of my neighbours in the early hours of the morning on more than one occasion. I prefer to have a window open at night (even in winter sometimes) but had no choice but to close it this week due to the aforementioned arguments, traffic and foxes copulating angrily. Do they copulate any other way? The point of all this being that when the alarm went off this morning at 6am I didn't hear it, or at least didn't have the idea to actually take the hint and wake up until 6.15am, by which point I was left with fifteen minutes to get out of the house and be on my way. These timings were in no small part influenced by the mishap last week which meant, due to missing a train, I had to detour to Southwark Park. It's amazing what you can do when motivated, even if you are a sleep-deprived zombie who is unsure of whether he is still dreaming or not. I got dressed, no doubt in clumsy fashion, and shuffled to the kitchen to make a flask of coffee to take with me, then brushed my teeth, dumped my kindle, ipod, GoPro and phone in the pack with everything else and left the flat.
Conscious that I was slightly behind schedule, I ran all the way to Ealing Broadway, feeling pretty good despite the lack of sleep and early start. At the station I found the District Line train and boarded. It left on time at 6.48am, and this week, thankfully, there were no delays, so that when it pulled in to Victoria I had plenty of time to find the platform and get on board the 7.39 to Dartford.
I drank some of the coffee I'd made earlier and read for the half an hour or so it took to get from Victoria to Welling. Getting off I knew which way to go having done my research earlier in the week via Google Maps and Streetview. I walked down the high street and turned right onto Danson Crescent, following it all the way to Danson Park, where I had a quick look at the map by the entrance and jogged uphill to look for the toilets in the

car park. I could already see some folk making their way slowly down the hill from the car park to the gathering area for the run, but I still had plenty of time. Following them soon afterwards I passed a large pond and garden and saw a group formed by the side of the lake, some people with dogs. I was now using compression shorts underneath normal running shorts. I hadn't used compression in running since my last ultramarathon in 2014. That was when the chronic sprain in my right foot (that's right - the 'Bad foot') reached its painful, nearly disastrous peak. Since getting some new compression shorts I found they did actually make my legs feel better during a run, giving more spring to my step, and hopefully helping to reduce muscle soreness after the longer runs. Unfortunately, the pair of running shorts I was wearing on top didn't have any pockets so I had to juggle my GoPro and phone while I took a couple of photos.

It wasn't long before the run director called for any parkrun newcomers and tourists to come over for a quick briefing. Besides myself there were a couple of tourists from Stratford-upon-Avon, Maidstone and Hilly Fields. Nice mix. After this quick talk it was time for the big pre-run briefing and everyone assembled in one big group. The RD informed us that there was a canoeing event on the lake, and that some (or possibly all) of them may be a bit anti-social so we were to be careful and advise them to maybe take up running where everyone tends to be friendly all of the time.

The Course

It was time for a short walk to the start line where we were very quickly unleashed. This week I was a little too far back, even though I thought I'd positioned myself in the right place. Maybe people had crept past me while I wasn't looking. Anyway, after a nice, steady start I began pushing ahead and getting through the pack. The route begins along the bottom of the lake, heading anti-clockwise, and turns left over first a small, twisting bridge where for some reason I lost my grip on the GoPro and it fell to the floor. I stopped briefly and managed to pick it up without it or me being trampled, then carried on along a walkway parallel to the lake and the road. This affords a great view over the lake, or at least I presume it does – on both laps I was either preoccupied with the GoPro or with my position in the pack. Past the lake the course heads uphill toward a car park then curves left and follows a tarmac path toward the impressive Danson House that stands looking down over the park. Toward the end the path dipped down between rows of flowers and then turned right at the bottom to go up another long hill to turn right at the top, down the road and then left into the forest section which was a welcome addition to the route, being scenic as well as downhill. On emerging from the forest there was a small grass section to cross to get back to the path that runs along the bottom of the park. Soon enough as I caught up with a couple of runners I passed a group of volunteers and uttered a gasping 'cheers!' I try to do this when I pass all volunteers to show my gratitude, though what I think I'm saying and what they actually hear coughed up from my heaving lungs could well be two different things.

It was then on to lap two which was actually easier than I expected. On the occasion when I had to speed up to get past people I would think *why don't I run this fast more often?* The belief being that I wasn't running as hard throughout the whole run as I could be. The problem is that while this may be partly true, it is also the kind of thinking that causes people to burn out long before they reach the finish line. Besides, for some reason I didn't feel in 'PB' mode today. I was more interested in just enjoying the run and the course which, to be fair, is more important. It's a run not a race, remember? And this isn't an excuse for what may be a slower time than last week. Honest.

Near the end of lap two I came off the path and ran on the grass toward the finishing funnel, trying to sprint and keep the GoPro steady at the same time – something that's as unnatural as it sounds. I still can't be bothered to use the headstrap though. I took my chip and had this and my barcode scanned then waited a while to film people coming in and chat to the run director. He filled me in on a bit of the background of Bexley Parkrun. He told me that when it started over four years ago they were getting numbers of around 40 to 50, then the last couple of years it was more like 200, and now it's even higher. He reckons a lot of recent press has helped. I can believe it. I'm hearing more and more about Parkrun lately, and not just because I'm running it every Saturday. People hear about Parkrun and ask 'I can run in my local park with others and get timed, but it's not a race? That's not a bad idea.' The run director also reminded me that 12$^{th}$ September will be Parkrun's 12$^{th}$ anniversary and local MPs are being encouraged to attend their local runs. Could be more good publicity. He then mentioned a new parkrun that should be starting up before the end of the year, and which would bring the total number of Greater London Parkruns to 46. *Oh*, I thought. *Bugger.* He asked if I would have to re-brand. I had actually thought about this recently. My thinking was that provided I completed the 45 parks I initially set out to run, I would be happy, but I would do any additional ones on top of that. To be able to say I was 'Lon-Done' I would probably have to do the new ones anyway. There was a chance I could be doing this forever.

Some radicalised canoeists then started some trouble with a few parkrunners so the RD went off to sort them out. Well, probably not, but it's a fun thought. I retrieved my bag, now with more to think about than I had expected, but very grateful for it, had a bit of flapjack and a drink and headed off toward the exit. It would be a long journey back home but it was well worth it. The weather had been a bit dull but Bexley had been anything but. The list of parkruns I wanted to re-visit was growing all the time. So many parkruns, so few Saturdays . . .

As I left the park I scowled at a dog that was relieving itself on the otherwise pristine statue of the great Ted Danson himself. At least I presumed it was Ted Danson . . .

Cheers.


Position: 48 out of 346
Time: 23 minutes, 37 seconds

I was expecting a slower time than the last few weeks – there were a few notable uphill sections on this course, I had a fairly slow, gradual start, and in general I didn't really feel like pushing myself, although I wasn't exactly hanging around either. It had been a very poor week for sleep too so this may have contributed. That said, I have noticed a gradual improvement in my running, and the 8 mile run I did on Wednesday night (part of my training for the Ealing half marathon) seemed to go pretty well. The foot was bad a couple of times this week, but it was pretty good today. All in all another great parkrun. Can there possibly be a bad one? The location for next week's Parkrun will be down to the randomizer again . . .

## 9. Barking
6th August, 2016
'Absolutely . . .'


Preamble

The 'randomizer' chose Barking early on in the week and, checking Google Maps, I saw it was another East London parkrun. Luckily it was fairly straightforward to get to from Ealing, but I was starting to worry that I was neglecting West London a bit. Before using the 'randomizer' app to choose the next parkrun, I was saving a couple of my local events for those occasions where I was running late, but there are plenty more in West London I need to run. Still, it's not up to me, it's up to the randomizer. That said, I can't complain about Barking parkrun. It didn't hurt that it was a spectacular summer morning, but the park is huge, with a long lake on one side, and plenty of twists and turns to make the two lap course interesting. I was surprised that there was a crowd of only 71 runners, but this might be standard for Barking. As usual they were a lively, friendly bunch, and the volunteers were terrific.

The alarm went off at 6.30am, though when I looked at the clock it was 6.32, so subconsciously I must have insisted on two more minutes. Either way, I got up, had breakfast, got dressed then had an agonizing few minutes waiting for the bathroom to be free. Normally I can't go to the toilet this early in the morning, but for someone reason my body fancied a change this week – the only week ever that someone else was up this early. Typical. Once (considerably) relieved I headed out of the flat close to 15 minutes behind schedule and ran all the way to Ealing Broadway station where I jumped on a Central Line train, leaving the station at around 7.35am. Luckily there were no holdups and my fears of getting to Barking late and having to sprint to catch the start of the run were unfounded. After changing at Mile End to a Hammersmith and City Line train, it was only 10 minutes to Barking where I turned left out of the station and followed the road down to Barking Park.

The weather was glorious – a beautiful, blue sky but not too hot. I managed to find my way first to the toilet block, then around the corner to where I found a few people already forming near the start. I had a drink and warmed up a little before the run director asked for anyone new to parkrun, or just to Barking Park, to assemble by him for the newcomers' briefing. After this there were a few more minutes before we all lined up near the start line.

In a way I had been preparing for this run all week. Last week at Bexley I had been in a more relaxed mood and just wanted to enjoy the parkrun and not worry too much about my time. This week I felt like I was on a mission. I had managed to lose a little weight recently and the long run home from central London on Thursday night (part of my prep for the Ealing Half Marathon in September), despite being a bit chaotic, hadn't left me with the tired, sore legs I'd been dreading. I had run home to Ealing from the Strand, via Green Park, Hyde Park, Holland Park (accidentally), then the Uxbridge Road through Shepherd's Bush and Acton. I had set myself a target of 10 miles, and at exactly that distance I stopped. I had my rucksack on my back with my clothes and shoes in, and the extra weight, along with getting a little lost, had made the run harder than expected, and even though I was still two miles from home when I finished I decided 10 miles was enough, so I caught the 207 bus the rest of the way home.

Encouraged by the fact that the 10 miler hadn't left me with aches and pains, I was confident of a new PB at Barking. With this in mind I positioned myself near the front of the group at the start line, just behind what I expected to be the lead runners. I had decided not to listen to music this week to see if it made a difference, so the iPod stayed in my bag near the finish line.


The Course

As the run director counted us down there was the familiar lurch forward, and I found myself with the front runners, watching the fastest two disappear out of sight almost straight away. I managed to stick with the other four or five for almost the whole of the first lap. From the tennis courts we headed down the tarmac path all the way to the end of the park where we curved around to the left and took a hairpin bend that brought us back on ourselves, now on the path alongside the lake. From here we could see the runners behind us on the path to the left, themselves heading toward the hairpin bend. We followed the lake all the way to the end of the park before turning left and coming back on ourselves again, this time winding through tree-lined paths until we passed a group of volunteers, cheering us on and pointing the way to the right, where the course heads out into the large open grass area of the park. The path curves around toward the far corner near the road, then turns left and follows the edge of the park, before abruptly turning left again and following a long avenue back toward the start area. I had been holding on to my fast pace (though I never actually checked my watch to see how fast I was going), and had been trying to keep it together until I got to the second lap. As I started on the second half of the run I still felt strong and just took each section as it came, giving myself several virtual checkpoints to aim toward rather than focussing solely on the finish line. This always helps, particularly if you're running out of your comfort zone and need to keep yourself from getting demoralised by objectives that seem too far off.

Eventually the avenue came around again. I knew several people were ahead of me, including a father and son team, but I couldn't be sure how close the finish line was to the end of the avenue, so didn't know when to start going all out. I sprinted about halfway down the avenue and was surprised to find the finish line across the path at the end of it. I realised I'd forgotten to film myself crossing the line, but it wasn't the end of the world – I knew I'd taken enough footage with the GoPro to make a video of the run. I took my token and considered collapsing on the grass or sitting on one of the logs nearby to recover, but didn't feel as bad as I'd expected, so I had my personal barcode and the finish token scanned, watched a few more runners finish, then headed off out of the park via the lake, to make my way back to Barking station where I bought I nice big vanilla latte at the coffee shop.

I really can't fault Barking parkrun. It's a great course that (surprise, surprise) I'd love to run again. Some great paths, a lake, some great running in the open. A really nice mix. And the weather was perfect. You'd have to be absolutely barking to miss it.


Position: 12 out of 71
Time: 22 minutes, 17 seconds (PB by 35 seconds)

I knew early on in the week that I had a good chance at a PB. And during the first lap of the run, finding myself with the front runners and staying with them, I knew that if I could just grit my teeth and stop myself from slowing down too much I wouldn't have a problem. I was hoping to get something like 22.30, and actually ending up with thirteen seconds better was amazing. If I was to run this course again I reckon I could get a better time. I would know what to expect and where to speed up (particularly on the approach to the finish line), but I'm very happy with the result. Another important factor is that there are no real inclines to speak of. In fact I can't remember any, save the slight downhill from the start toward the lake. Either way, what a way to smash that PB.

## 10. Fulham Palace
10th September, 2016
'Things fall apart . . . Then come back together again.'


Preamble

In the week following the Barking parkrun I was a little overzealous with my interval training, and this, coupled with not giving my legs enough rest, caused a muscle tear in my left thigh. It started as a twinge during an easy run on the day after the interval training, but then grew more and more painful until I had no choice but to stop and walk home. I knew this would take at least a couple of weeks to sort itself out, but still needed my parkrun fix, so I decided to take a break from the 45 Parks challenge the next Saturday and get some volunteering in.
Checking their volunteer pages I saw that Gunnersbury and Northala Fields (both local) had plenty of volunteers for the next run, and I was almost resigned to having a Saturday off (oh no!), when the run director for Southwark parkrun suggested via Twitter that I help out at Southwark. So that was that. I was glad I went too, as volunteering is not only worthwhile but great fun. I stood by one of the turns on the course, ensuring everyone went the right way, clapping and shouting encouragement every now and again. Once or twice a runner would shout their gratitude between breaths as they passed, and I made a mental note then to shout out the occasional word of thanks on future runs.
The following week I'd planned to visit friends in Milton Keynes, and run the parkrun there. In the days prior I was concerned I wouldn't get around without making the injury worse, but luckily the friend I was running with didn't do a lot of running, and wasn't interested in running fast anyway, so I stuck with him and we slowly made our way around the course in an easy (for me at least) 35 minutes. The Milton Keynes course around Willen Lake is great. It's mainly flat but has a great zig-zagging climb half way around and gives you great views across the lake for most of its length. At the end there is a long straight section slightly uphill toward the finish, where my friend managed a sprint, but I didn't, knowing it wouldn't do my thigh any good. I was very pleased that despite the injury I was able

to run steadily (if slowly), and was confident that I could continue the 45 Parks challenge the following week, provided I continued to reign myself in for a while and give the thigh a chance to heal properly before even thinking about PBs again.

A few days later I decided to do an easy run after work, following the Ealing Half Marathon course for a couple of miles. I managed to make it up and down one hill, but before I got to the really steep one the pain in my thigh flared up and I had to give in and walk back home. This was very frustrating and even though Milton Keynes had gone ok, I knew I would just have to avoid running for a couple of weeks. So over the next two Saturdays I hiked two more sections of the London Loop, not doing anything strenuous, just around ten miles each time. At the end of the second day I found myself within reach of Riddlesdown parkrun, and wondered if I'd be fit to do it in the next couple of weeks before doing the next section of the London Loop. But before that I decided I'd try a more local run as most of the 45 parkruns I'd done so far seemed to be in East London.

In the days leading up to the Fulham Palace parkrun the thigh had been ok, and I had done a slow, easy 5k during the week to see how it felt and it had held up, though I was left with the feeling that if I had done any more I might well have had a relapse. On the Saturday morning I woke, groaning at the dull sky outside, then got myself ready, leaving the flat later than planned to walk the ten minutes or so to Ealing Broadway station where I caught a District Line train to Earl's Court and changed to a train heading to Putney Bridge. I was worried that I would be late, but luckily I got to Putney Bridge with time to spare and followed some other runners, guessing they too were headed to the parkrun. There was a very light drizzle in the air, but the heavy rain didn't come until the afternoon.

On reaching Bishop's Park I saw lots of flags and marquees and saw that a Thames Path Challenge was in progress. People wearing numbers and small backpacks were milling around, and after the parkun while I was heading back to the station there were lines of people wearing charity t-shirts obviously taking part in what must have been a huge event. I was worried that this might have meant the parkrun was cancelled, and cursed myself for not checking the news section of the Fulham Palace parkrun website, but on reaching the start point I saw the parkrun was, thankfully, going ahead as planned. Apparently both events had coexisted happily for the last couple of years.

I dropped my bag and did a few stretches before it was time for the newcomers' briefing and then the main run briefing. After this we all walked as a group to the start point near the children's play area and I made sure I was nowhere near the start as this wouldn't have helped the injury.

The Course

I tucked into the pack between the middle and the back and we were soon moving off, me taking care not to get too excited and run faster than I should. I was wearing a thigh support I had bought a week ago, unsure as to whether it would help or hinder me, but willing to give it a go as I felt I needed all the help I could get. In the end I think it may well have been the most important factor in me getting around the course without doing more damage, and intend to keep using it until the thigh is properly healed. I only really sped up a couple of times during the whole run, and only temporarily just so I could either get out of someone's way or to overtake someone who was in mine. I did also speed up a little as I approached the finish, but this wasn't for very long.

The course starts near the north end of Bishop's Park and follows the perimeter path in an anti-clockwise direction first heading up to toward the football stadium and turning left to head toward the river. On a brighter day the Thames would have been a much more welcome sight, but it was still nice to be running alongside the river for a good stretch. We passed the Thames Path Challenge area again with people engaged in warm-up exercises, before finally turning left off the riverside path and left again by Fulham Palace and heading back toward the meeting area where the finish funnel had been set up, turning right and then left again by the children's playground to enter the second lap.

The thigh was holding up well, in fact I wasn't feeling anything like the pain and discomfort I had been expecting. I really wanted to run faster, but I knew this would be a bad idea, and so just hung back and enjoyed the run. As I came to the finish funnel I slowed and stopped, not exactly out of breath but feeling like I'd done some exercise, and also feeling very happy that I was back to parkrun. It wasn't going to be a very fast time, but I wasn't fussed about that. Finishing in one piece had always been the primary objective.

Position: 210 out of 345
Time: 27 minutes, 53 seconds

So that's 5 minutes 36 seconds slower than my PB of a month ago. A massive gap, but I'm just happy that I was able to get around the course. Having an injury that stops you from doing the sport/exercise you love is incredibly frustrating, but once the initial healing is done and the point comes where you can do that activity with support or at a slower, steadier pace, you know that you are making progress, and you no longer have to force yourself to avoid that activity altogether. The important thing for me now is to ensure I can keep doing parkrun. This will mean using a support until my thigh is back to normal, but I'm ok with that. In fact 27 minutes, 53 seconds is fine by me. Roll on next Saturday!

## 11. Riddlesdown
17th September, 2016
'Up on the downs'


Preamble

Last week's run at Fulham Palace had been encouraging – wearing the thigh support for my injury had allowed me to run at a slow but steady pace, and there had been no sign of a relapse afterward. I had one training run during the week on Wednesday night, just three miles around a nearby park, and though the thigh felt a lot stiffer and tighter, I got through it, again with no damage done. I think running at the end of the day compared to the start makes a difference, and I probably didn't do enough stretching and warming up beforehand. Either way I was happy to give Riddlesdown a go and see how it went, once again wearing thigh support and compression.
My alarm had been set for the depressing time of 5.45am, but this meant I would have half an hour to get ready and then get to Ealing Broadway station to catch a 6.39 train. As it turned out, (surprise, surprise) I was running late when I finally got out of the flat and got to the station just to see the train I needed pulling away. I boarded the next train and eight minutes later we were moving. I checked the travel details again and saw that I should be ok. My plan was to take a train from Victoria to Sanderstead, then catch a bus down the road to Hamsey Green where it was a short walk to the start of the parkrun. Even if I missed the train I needed from Victoria I should still be able to catch the next one and be there on time.
The train reached Oxford Circus and I jumped off and headed to the Victoria Line platform, arriving at Victoria Station several minutes later. I rushed to the main terminal with about three minutes to catch the original train I'd be hoping to get, only to find on looking at the arrivals and departures board that the train had been cancelled due to staff shortages. Looks like I'd been destined to get a later train after all. It crossed my mind then that maybe the later trains going in that direction might be cancelled to, so until the 7.53 train showed up on the board I

scanned the other destinations, already planning an alternative parkrun should Riddlesdown be unachievable. I was hoping I didn't have to go somewhere else as I had a specific reason for choosing Riddlesdown – two weeks ago I'd finished hiking a section of the London Loop right next to Riddlesdown, and I had planned to do the parkrun there this week, then hike the final section of London Loop to Kingston. I considered Bromley as a possible alternative though, thinking that I could maybe get a bus to Riddlesdown afterwards to continue the walk and return there at a later date to do the parkrun.

I went over to the travel information desk and asked the lady if she thought the next train (toward East Grinstead) was likely to be cancelled and she said it should be fine. I also realised at that point that rather than getting off at Sanderstead I could just carry on to Riddlesdown Station. It looked like a fair walk from there to the parkrun, but might still be a safer bet than getting the bus.

At 7.53 the train left Victoria, and in only twenty minutes or so it pulled in at Riddlesdown, just as a light rain began to fall. The sky had been a dark grey all morning, but the weather forecast hadn't predicted any significant rainfall. I had brought my rain jacket just in case though, and was prepared to run with it if necessary. From the station I checked the map on my phone to ensure I was going in the right direction and started a long slog uphill to get onto the downs themselves, then found Riddlesdown road and followed it and a few side paths all the way to the site of the parkrun, taking it in turns to run and walk to get warmed up.

I was worried I would run out of time, and at around ten to nine I emerged from a path into a wide field at the top of the downs, looking around for any sign of activity. I noticed a couple of runners off to my left and followed the same direction they were headed in, toward the corner of a field where there seemed to be a marshal point. A few other people had arrived by the time I got there, and soon there was a large group chatting, warming up and getting ready to go. Luckily the rain was holding off and it was just cool enough to be comfortable, though there was a pretty strong wind. A very kind volunteer agreed to look after my bag and take it with her to her marshal point. We were given the run briefing then it was time to go. I noticed the lady giving the briefing whip off her jacket and join the throng as we moved off, which I thought was great.

The Course

We started off running flat across the top of the downs with great views to the left across the valley towards Kenley Common, before turning slightly left then right and continuing straight on until there was an almost hairpin bend sending us up a steep bank to a right turn and a woodland path at the top. We followed this great path for a fair while, before it opened out into fields again, and followed a boundary path to the left that ended at a marshal who pointed to the right, the direction of the finish funnel. It wasn't even the end of the first lap yet though, so I carried on, following a group of three as we turned right at a hedge and ran along the other side of the field until eventually turning left and heading back toward the start flag.

The first lap had been great and I was pleased that the injury in my left thigh hadn't flared up. In fact I was confused that it had been so comfortable. The thigh support was no doubt doing its job, but I had still expected to be slowed down by the injury. Through the second lap I found I was able to speed up occasionally without any pain, and could no doubt have run faster, though I still wasn't comfortable with taking any kind of risk. As I made the final turn toward the finish funnel (the second lap is shorter than the first so it finishes before you reach the start again) I avoided sprinting and just sped up a little, happy that I had finished a few minutes faster than last week. A significant improvement. I took my token and walked toward the small tent that had been set up by the volunteers to get the token and my barcode scanned, then headed back to the start to see if I could meet up with the marshal who had looked after my bag for me. At first I couldn't see her and had a horrible feeling she'd taken a different route to the finish and was waiting for me there (I couldn't have faced turning and going all that way back again), but then saw her appear over the crest of the hill and jogged to meet her, thanking her for being so helpful.

Now there was just the small matter of a 23 mile hike from Riddlesdown to Kingston to finish the London Loop...


Position: 35 out of 121
Time: 24 minutes, 04 seconds

I wasn't really expecting the result to be that much better than at Fulham Palace the week before, but a difference of around three minutes was fantastic. The ground had been a lot more technical too compared to the flat tarmac path at Fulham Palace. That said, there were less turns to negotiate and the ground was softer, so this may well have had an impact (no pun intended). I remembered while writing this that I have a half marathon to do next Sunday, a distance I'm not really prepared for. I want to do a parkrun next Saturday too, so that, coupled with the long hike might actually help me get around. There may have to be some walking though.

## 12. Old Deer Park
24th September, 2016
'Oh dear'


Preamble

I was up at 6.45am and raring for action. After a quick breakfast and having put on my compression shorts, thigh support and brand new parkrun t-shirt (with 'Gunnersbury' printed on the front), I left the house at about 7.30am to jog down the road to the station where I caught a 7.50am District Line train to Turnham Green and changed to a train to Richmond. I was surprised at how quick I got there having had problems getting to Richmond in the past, but I reached the station at about 8.15am, giving me plenty of time to get to Old Deer Park. I used the loo then left the station and crossed the road, heading down an alley to a car park and beyond that a pedestrian crossing bridge. I found Pools on the Park, the swimming pool/sports centre and wandered around to the main field, checking my phone to work out exactly where the start would be. I seemed to be one of the first there, so I jogged over to the start area, dropped my bag by a tree and did some warm ups along the path by the road.
After a quick jog around and some stretches I waited for the run briefing. It was Old Deer Park's 300th run, so it was good to be there at such a milestone. When the briefing was over everyone walked to the start line by the tennis courts. The run director counted down and let everyone go. During the warm up I'd had to adjust my thigh support as it kept slipping down my leg, and frustratingly the same thing happened at the start of the run. Not only would it have looked bizarre to everyone else if I'd left it as it was, but it could have tripped me up, or at least made the whole run more of a challenge than it ought to be. I stopped and tried to refasten it but it was no use. I could now either just let it slip and be either useless or a restriction while I ran, or take it off. I took it off and ran with it in my left hand, intending to throw it in the general direction of my bag when I finished the first lap. Great.

The Course

The course is very straightforward, and for the most part follows the perimeter of the park in a clockwise direction. It first approaches and passes the gathering point near the road, then turns sharp right and heads parallel to the road, passing through trees for a while before turning right at a marshal point and following some strategically placed flags to reach the other end of the park where it turns right again by the treeline and continues for quite a long straight on flat grass before returning to the tennis courts and turning right to begin the next lap. Having lost time trying to fix my support in place I was playing catch up for the first lap and running faster than I'd wanted to. On passing the start again the run director – a very helpful chap indeed - reached out and took the support from me, saving me time in finding somewhere to fling it, and from having to run the rest of the course with it (it's quite a large item). The second lap was still pretty fast, though it felt like I was flagging toward the end, and I took it a bit easier on the third lap, not wanting to get out of breath.

After passing through the finishing funnel I retrieved my support and had a drink. I decided it must have been the compression shorts I'd been wearing underneath that had caused the support to keep slipping, being made of very smooth material. I had the Ealing half marathon to do the next day which I hadn't properly trained for because of the thigh injury, so I decided not to wear these compression shorts, just the support on its own. A shame really as they were orange and (almost) went with the apricot Parkrun t-shirt. I had managed to get through most of the run without the support, which was encouraging, but that was 3 miles. The 13 miles of the half marathon would be a different matter altogether.

Position: 25 out of 82
Time: 24 minutes, 08 seconds

It was nowhere close to my best time for the year so far, but I wasn't bothered. I was still recovering from the thigh injury so I wasn't expecting any spectacular results just yet. Twenty-four minutes was fine by me. I would bring the time down gradually over the next few weeks, provided the thigh held out, not to mention the thigh support.

# 13. Pymmes
1st October, 2016
'O'clock'


Preamble

In a way I was dreading the Ealing Half Marathon last week. My thigh still wasn't back to normal, and because of the injury I hadn't been able to train properly. Nevertheless I managed to complete the half marathon in just under an hour and fifty-seven minutes. The beginning was great and I was loving it, but although I remained strong for most of the distance, I was really flagging by the end and praying for it all to finish. To my amazement the only time I stopped to walk was for about half a minute, less than a mile from the finish. All in all I was amazed at what I had achieved, though I knew a lot of the credit had to go to the thigh support. What an incredible thing it was. I took it easy during the week, wanting to be recovered for the next parkrun at Pymmes. I certainly wasn't intending to miss it.
I woke at 5.50am, about twenty-five minutes before the alarm, but couldn't feel smug about beating it, as I was too tired, and surprised that it wasn't the middle of the night. I lay in bed for a while then got up, not expecting it to still be dark outside. Once again time disappeared while getting ready but I was still able to get out of the house for about 6.50am as planned. The Central Line train I wanted was waiting for me at Ealing Broadway station, so I boarded and sat down to read my Kindle, finding soon afterwards that I was starting to feel sleepy again. Not good, so I listened to some music instead. I had intended to get a fairly early night the night before, but half an hour spent pulling the drawstring back through my compression shorts, followed by an ultimately fruitless hunt for a Daddy Long-Legs that had invited itself in, meant I ended up getting to bed an hour later than planned. I was also worried that I might be tempted to run too fast and risk injuring myself after I'd run a half marathon the previous Sunday, but I felt generally fit.
At Oxford Circus I changed to the Victoria Line and headed north a few stops to Seven Sisters where I needed to catch an overland train to Silver

Street Station which was opposite Pymmes Park. Standing on the platform I was reassured to see a bright blue sky. There had been talk of rain but I was hoping it would have the good manners to wait until after parkrun which, thankfully it did.

The Cheshunt train arrived a few minutes later and it was then a short haul north to Silver Street. Taking the steps down from the platform to street level I could see the park opposite, and headed right down the road until I found an entrance. It was only 8.15am so I had plenty of time to take some photos and video with the phone and GoPro and get some warming up done. It was a great time of the day to be in a park, seeing a light mist about and rays of sunshine through the trees.

At about 8.50am I wandered over to the start. There were only three or four people there, but by 8.55am a good huddle of runners had assembled. I noticed a couple of people wearing the increasingly trendy apricot Parkrun t-shirts, and was surprised to see one chap wearing the same 'Gunnersbury' one as me. This turned out to be Tom Corbett, who was a member of the Ealing Eagles running club, and who had taken part in an impressive number of parkruns all over the country and abroad too. We chatted for a while about parkrun tourism and he recommended checking out Tring. He went on to win this particular parkrun in a fantastic time of 18 minutes 12 seconds. I caught sight of him a few times during the run and he was so far ahead he may well have lapped me if there had been a fourth lap.


The Course

At 9am we headed to the start point, and after a brief introduction from the run director Austen Slattery, including some running milestones for a few Pymmes regulars, it was time to move. The Pymmes course is a straightforward one, but no bad thing for that. It involves three laps of the park, with the finishing funnel being at the gathering point, a short distance from the start. You begin by running to the north end of the park, anti-clockwise, and turning left at the end to run along one of the two shorter sides before turning left again and heading towards what looks like (from above) a bicycle-shaped lake (if the bicycle had been involved in an accident that is), where you veer to the right in a curve and head between trees towards the road, taking a left which soon brings you to a small pond. The sun was right in front of us here and very bright, but the rain was still held at bay. The young chap who had been in front of me for the whole run was still keeping his lead, and although I was tempted to try and overtake, I was worried that I might strain myself and cause some post-half marathon damage. I know – excuses, excuses.

Beyond the pond the path takes a sharp left, then right by a building and continues on around the park, passing the lake again before passing the children's playground, the exercise equipment, and the finish funnel.

I had checked my time on the first lap and had been keeping a pace of around seven and a half minutes per mile which was fast enough considering I wasn't at peak fitness. The second and third lap were no easier than the first though, and I was starting to flag on the third, but thankfully the young chap in front of me paced me to the finish in a decent time. As usual I had been filming the run with my GoPro camera, but made the same mistake when coming through the finish funnel that I'd made in the past – turning the camera off when I thought I was turning it on. So I missed the finish. Never mind. I had my barcode and token scanned, had a drink and then headed off to the station for the journey home. I was glad I'd brought my rain jacket with me as it had finally started to rain. Not the first time the weather seemed to have waited for parkrun to finish before turning bad. Very considerate.

Position: 13 out of 38
Time: 23 minutes

Considering I'm still recovering from the half marathon last Sunday (which I had to stop training for over a month ago due to the thigh injury), this isn't too bad a time. I am now less than a minute away from my PB of 22 minutes 17 seconds. It is starting, finally, to come back into view. Who knows, maybe in a week or two I will be going sub-22 minutes. But regardless of whether the thigh has pulled itself together or not (not sure if that's merely figurative) it's bound to hurt.

## 14. Canons Park
8th October, 2016
'Inaugural'


Preamble

As with a couple of weeks ago, this would be a busy weekend for running. I had the parkrun on the Saturday followed by a 10k race in Edmonton on the Sunday. It seemed like a good idea until I realised, waking up rather groggily at 6.15am on the morning of the parkrun, that my Sunday morning 'lie in' would be getting up at 7.15am, followed by a train journey across London to run a fast 10k. Not really a habit I wanted to get into, but I did like the sound of the 10k, and true enough 'Run the River' did turn out to be excellent. But back to the parkrun . . .
This was the first Canons Park parkrun, and I was keen to take part in the inaugural event as I hadn't been to one before. It did mean that my 45 Parks challenge had now become 46 Parks (rendering the three t-shirts I'd had printed obsolete) but I wouldn't let that bother me – it meant parkrun was still growing, and that was something to celebrate. Sliding out of bed and wondering where, when and indeed 'who' I was, I (gradually) woke up, ate breakfast and left the flat at about 7am to give myself plenty of time to get to the park. I had to catch a Central Line train to Bond Street, then a Jubilee Line train north to Canons Park, getting there at around 8.30am. This meant I had plenty of time to warm up so I took advantage of it, stretching and jogging along the path not far from the King George V Memorial Gardens. The sky was very grey, and light rain occasionally fell, but nothing really worth worrying about. The crowd was slowly gathering by the cafe, and by 8.55am there were over a hundred keen runners waiting to get stuck in. An entertaining brief was given by the run director, correctly pointing out that we were all first-timers and therefore needed to listen to the brief. Then we were guided toward the start line and were soon off and running.


The Course

From the start line the first stretch is across grass, with the crowd spread quite wide, then things narrow as the course joins the long path that heads roughly south-east towards the Donnefield Avenue entrance, but taking a left turn before getting there and following the perimeter path by the tennis courts and alongside the running track of the activity centre for a fairly long straight before taking a sharp turn left, then left again by Whitchurch Lane, coming back on a path parallel to the one by the activity centre. This was a great stretch as it gave not only a view toward the runners ahead of me, but also of those behind me. Following the path by the trees for a while, the course soon took a sharp right into the trees on a fantastic woodland path where, not long after entering the woods, the run organisers had put a hi-viz vest on a low branch to make runners aware of the hazard. Either that or the tree itself was a volunteer, which would surely be a first for Parkrun.

The wooded path continued on for a good while and was probably my favourite section of the course, even if it did slope upwards towards the end demanding a little more effort to maintain my pace. At the top of the slope the course turns left out of the trees and across grass to a tarmac path that runs along the front wall of the memorial gardens and returns to the gathering point, just before the start line.

For the second lap I was able to maintain my pace of around 7 minutes 30 seconds, and the same for the third lap. I came through the finish funnel not really worrying about my time, but focussing more on the fact that I'd been part of an inaugural parkrun event, which was actually pretty cool. I then had to run another three miles to Harrow and Wealdstone station to get a train (which I missed by about ten seconds) to Bletchley for a friend's birthday.


Position: 20 out of 117
Time: 22 minutes 50 seconds.

So I am ten seconds closer to my 5k PB. I'm getting there fairly slowly after recovering from the hip injury. I don't want to be aggressive about beating my best time, and I know that if I keep up the training I should get there naturally. The 10k race I did in Edmonton the next day was a challenge. I ran it at roughly the same pace as the parkrun, so it was like running two of them one after the other, but there didn't seem to be any issues, certainly not from the hip or the ankle (which hasn't been a problem for quite a while now, touch wood). There was a lot of teeth-gritting involved, but it does prove that there is always more in the tank than I think. The mad sprint finish to the end on the running track proved that too.

## 15. Valentines Park

15th October, 2016
'For the sheer love of it'

Preamble

Today was going to be a mad attempt to beat last week's time by a minute, beat my PB by around ten seconds, and get below the 21 minute threshold for my 5k. Well, that didn't happen but I did beat my PB, so it was by no means a disappointment.

I had an early night last night, but it didn't help as I didn't get to sleep until 1am, waking at 3am to wonder what on Earth was going on, then again at 6.15am when the alarm went off. At first I thought it had to be a joke as it felt like I'd only just closed my eyes. Nope. It was cold too, so treacherous thoughts of giving up this week's parkrun as a bad idea and climbing back into a warm bed started to creep into my head. But I got up, went to the bathroom, then made breakfast. Once again . . . <sigh> I lost track of time so that I didn't end up leaving the flat until about 7.15am, when it had meant to be 7.10am at the latest. I hot-footed it (walked actually) to Ealing Broadway Station, then boarded the waiting (it was very patient as it didn't leave for another seven minutes) Central Line train toward Hainault.

This meant I was actually in danger of getting to Valentines late, or worse – missing the parkrun altogether, an idea that filled me with dread. Travelling all the way across London to miss a run is a terrible thought. I don't know what I'd do if it happened. Run around the park on my own, I suppose, but it would be a sad, bitter run, the complete antithesis of Parkrun. Anyway, let's not think about that.

I pondered my clothing choices while on the train and realised that I was right not to bother with track pants. I can tolerate cold legs, so shorts were fine, even though the morning was a lot colder than I had expected. The train finally deposited me at Gants Hill at about 8.35am and I soon found myself in a subway where I took the wrong exit and got lost, before checking my phone and getting myself back on track. I didn't have a lot of time so this was annoying. I found the road I was after and started jogging toward Valentines Park, soon finding an entrance and seeing other people in running gear. I felt confident that I wasn't as short of time as I thought I was. I jogged on down the path, by the side of a pond and then toward the gathering point for the walk. I was encouraged to see a large group already assembled, but relieved that the run brief hadn't started yet. I dumped my bag, did some brief stretching then joined the crowd near the start line.

I had decided to give the GoPro headstrap another go today, but I was running late and to get it set up properly needs a bit of calibration with my phone, so I decided to just hold the camera in my hand as usual. This can be a pain, and I was beginning to wish I could just run without a camera, which is probably why I wanted to try the headstrap again, as even though you can feel it up there, you can just leave it to its own devices and concentrate on running.

The run director gave us a quick brief, then there was the familiar surge forward accompanied by the sound of watches beeping and dozens of shoes hitting the tarmac.

The Course

The course begins with a straight section from the start, parallel to Valentines Park Boating Lake, before taking a left turn near the exit to Cranbrook Road. There is then another straight section following the park's perimeter path, turning left at the top path near the car park, and following the long path north-eastwards until it meets Melbourne Road where it takes a sharp left to follow the edge of a field which (going by Google Maps) looks like it's seen a staggering amount of activity. Just beyond here, by Valentines Café, and close to the start once more, the route turns right to head between trees before turning left along another tree-lined path next to a field I saw when I arrived at the park. There were what looked like Canada Geese there, some chasing each other around while others seemed to just stare blankly at the runners. We soon came to another left turn taking us over a bridge next to the pond, before the path curved right, then left toward Emerson road. There was then another left along a path that soon drew alongside the tennis courts.

We passed the bandstand and were tantalisingly close to the start again, but there was another lap to do, so on we went. The second lap went as well as can be expected. I didn't exert myself as much as I may have been able to, and I think that's the challenge I have to overcome if I want to get below 22 minutes – pushing myself beyond my comfort zone.

At the end of the second lap I was a bit confused as to when to turn left to head towards the finish, but I soon found the path and set my sights on the finish funnel, putting on a last spurt to try to make up lost seconds. I could have done more, I realised, but was more than happy to stop there. I knew I'd set a good time, even if it wasn't a PB. I would have to wait and see. As usual I forgot to stop my watch when I finished.

While getting ready to leave I chatted with another runner, telling her about my 46 parks tourism, and getting some good advice from her re: choosing winter parkruns. It hadn't occurred to me that the courses on grass were likely to get boggy. Worth remembering.

I had planned to get some more miles in after the parkrun, running to Leyton Station to catch the Central Line back to Ealing Broadway. This involved a run through residential streets to cross the North Circular, followed by a run along the lakes in Wanstead Park. Not a bad stretch at all.

Position: 18 out of 189
Time: 22 minutes 08 seconds.

So I beat my PB by 9 seconds. That's actually pretty good since I had only been creeping up on the PB over the last few weeks. I'm happy with that. Maybe next week I can enter undiscovered country and get below 22 minutes. I had decided during the week that from now on I would alternate between choosing a parkrun and selecting one at random. I was looking forward to running Osterley Park as it was local and I used to run around there some years ago, or Harrow for the same reasons. Spoiled for choice.

## 16. Osterley Park
22nd October, 2016
'Winter is coming'

Preamble

Another cold, dark morning, but as the run director at today's parkrun reminded me – it's still only autumn. I have all those lovely, properly cold winter parkruns to look forward to. But this was cold enough for now. I got up and silenced the alarm before it could get anywhere near its crescendo and put some coffee on while I sorted through the pile of clothes I'd dumped on the chair the night before. I wore the compression shorts again, with the thigh support over the top (I still needed it as it turned out) running shorts, a compression t-shirt and another t-shirt over the top. I also wore a fleece (I took it off before the run) and track pants with zips on the bottom of each leg so they can be taken off without removing your running shoes.
After a smoothie, Danish pastry, bowl of cereal and coffee (I know, it's a bit much), I left the flat late (surprise, surprise) at about 8.10am and ran the half mile or so to Northfields Station where I caught a busy Piccadilly Line train to Osterley. Off the train I soon caught sight of a couple in running gear and watched them head off down the road. I used to live in nearby Isleworth and ran around Osterley Park a lot, so I was looking forward to returning after several years. I turned off the busy A4 and walked down Thornbury Road to the end and the entrance to Osterley Park. This is where both cars and foot traffic access the park. Walking along the path I could see a light mist on the fields on either side and dew on the grass. If this wasn't winter, it was pretty close.
The car park at the end of the long avenue between the fields was filling up. When I reached the lake I could see many more runners making their way toward Osterley House, located to the north of the lake, facing the greater expanse of the park. I found a spot to take off my fleece and track pants, have a drink and stretch, before leaving my bag near the finish and getting ready to join everyone else as we wandered down the path to the start by the lake. After the routine introduction by the run director (during

which a nearby bell rang out the hour) we were off to tackle three laps of the Osterley Park course. I know how big the park is, and I'm pretty sure you could make a one-lap course but, presumably due to restrictions by the owners, it may be that only certain parts of the park can be used for this purpose. Either that or it's for health and safety reasons. That said, the course is a good one. I had been hoping that the two or three long sections would allow me to get some speed up and beat last week's time of 22 minutes 8 seconds, but given how uneven (and wet) the ground is in some places, coupled with the fact that my legs didn't feel too fresh, it became apparent about halfway around that this wouldn't be a PB week. Either way I was able to enjoy the course (particularly the wooded sections with its treacherous tree roots) and still push myself.

The Course

The course begins at the lake, turning right by Osterley House and taking the long, straight drive all the way to the gate at the bottom that opens into Osterley lane where the course turns right and follows the lane all the way to a marshal who points the way into the trees for a hairpin turn to the right, almost bringing the runners back on themselves. This section, through trees is where you will find several tree roots sprayed with bright paint to make them stand out. This is essential too as I'm pretty sure if they had been obscured I'd have gone flying and maybe ended up in the nearby lake.
After a while the path emerges from the trees and heads straight across the open grass of the main body of the park, before eventually turning right onto the gravel by the house and starting on the second lap. I knew I was pretty fast on the first lap, but at the same time not quite fast enough, and for the next two laps I was just about able to maintain that same pace, not dropping back too much, but not making up for lost time either. Coming to the finish I could see a few people on the floor and sat on the steps of the house. Maybe that's what I'm doing wrong – I'm not running so fast and hard that I'm a wreck by the end of the run. Finishing and being able to stay standing is, perhaps, a sign of failure.
Still, it's only a run.

Position: 27 out of 115
Time: 22 minutes 39 seconds

A slower time this week, possibly due to the terrain but also, I think, due to my legs not feeling great. This may have been due to the run to Northfields station before the run, but may also have been due to the 7.5 mile run I did on Wednesday night. If I didn't rest enough after that, the legs might not have been on top form. Still, who knows, maybe I just underestimated Osterley Park. A great course though. Look forward to getting back there at some point.

## 17. Hilly Fields

29th October, 2016
'The clue is in the name'

Preamble

Love and hate. Sometimes a parkrun course can inspire both. I'd had a cold all week, so getting myself up and out of bed at 6.15am was challenging to say the least. Almost surreal in fact. I'd had a good sleep though, thanks to the Night Nurse, so I was able to just about resist the massive gravitational pull of my bed once I was out of it. But although the cold had an effect on my run, it wasn't the overriding factor in me not getting a personal best.
It was another dark Saturday morning. I made coffee had some cereal, then addressed the huge pile of running clothes I'd assembled the night before. As it turned out it wasn't as cold outside as I had expected, but having every possibility catered for is always a good thing, so I had a fold-up rain jacket with me as well. This week I had decided not to wear the thigh support and see how it went. The injury hadn't been playing up in the last few weeks and I had a feeling that last week at Osterley the support had actually held me back rather than helped me. As it turned out I didn't have a problem with the thigh at all this time, and it definitely felt like it was almost back to normal.
I left the flat at 7.05am and walked to Ealing Broadway Station where I caught a Central Line train to Bond Street. I read my Kindle and found myself feeling pretty drowsy. I put this mainly down to being ill and getting up early, but reading wasn't helping, so I listened to music instead. At Bond Street I changed to the Jubilee Line, catching a train to Canada Water where I jumped on an overland train to Brockley.
The journey was quicker than expected and when I got off the train at Brockley I checked my phone to make sure I was on the right side of the tracks, then walked down to the main Brockley Road and turned right, following the road for several minutes before turning left onto Adelaide Avenue and following it up to Hilly Fields. Wow. Obviously, given its name, I wasn't expecting this park to be flat, but the slope before me still came

as a surprise. It was entirely possible that the course kept to flat sections of the park . . . Yeah, right. I followed the footpath up toward the café, seeing other runners arriving and warming up. I used the loo then dropped my bag on a bench facing the Hilly Fields stone circle (placed there to celebrate the millennium). I stripped off the fleece, base layer and track pants and did some stretching. There wasn't much time left before the run and again I hadn't left myself ample time for warming up (just one of several excuses I have lined up for this week's disappointing result), but I had a jog around the stone circle, then headed off down the path to find a large group of runners gathered by the tennis courts. A few minutes later we were walking back toward the café and the start line. The run director gave us a brief, and we were off.

The Course

I felt good to begin with as we headed forward, then gradually twisted downhill past the college and toward the road at the bottom. This was a fairly long downhill section which turned right at the bottom and followed a path along the edge of the park, parallel to Montague Avenue, and heading up toward the bowls club, and the top of the hill via a couple of (for me at least) gruelling uphill sections. To be fair these stretches were brief and broken up, but I struggled for some reason, maybe the lack of warm up or the lurgy. The course continued around the park, passing the stone circle until it arrived once more at the tennis courts where it was time for the second of the three laps. We headed downhill again and I was actually hopeful now that I knew what to expect, except that the second lap wasn't the same as the first. Instead of turning right at the bottom and following the outside path again, coloured markers directed us uphill quite sharply (my memory might be exaggerating the gradient somewhat). This not only took me by surprise but also almost drained me of everything I had left, which wasn't much to be honest (I really was having a bad run), but I pushed on and made it around the rest of that and the next lap. I have to give the course designer credit for having that slight change to the course after the first lap. It may have made it harder (for me at least) but it also makes the course more interesting. Imagine taking it further and having a course that changes every lap. That would be really confusing to newcomers, but great fun.
Arriving back at the tennis courts near the end of the third lap I was hoping the finish funnel was close, but I could now see the runners ahead

of me turning left and taking the downhill path again. Oh God. For a moment I thought maybe I'd accidentally started an unnecessary fourth lap, but no, this was all part of the course, so I gritted my teeth and ran around to the other side of the park and then took the straight back toward the finish, very glad that the run was over and done with.

This run was tough. I would say Hilly Fields can be a challenging course if you've never run it before and are used to running flat courses. No doubt local runners who have run Hilly Fields several times are used to it, but tourists like me can easily be caught out. The only other course I've run that I could compare to it in terms of uphill is Ludlow in Shropshire, though I've heard there are more challenging ones. But although it's tough I really like it. It doesn't make running easy, but that's not a bad thing. I imagine that if you can master Hilly Fields you can master any parkrun. Some of the times people have clocked on this course are very impressive indeed. How they do it I don't know.

Position: 49 out of 192
Time: 23 minutes 5 seconds.

Well, considering the undulating (understatement) course, my cold and the lack of warm up, I think I did pretty well. Just over twenty-three minutes is better than I was expecting as I panted my way around Hilly Fields park. I just need to get rid of this cold, do some more distance and speed training and choose a nice flat course, maybe one I'm already familiar with.

## 18. Harrow
5th November, 2016
'Remember, remember . . .'

Preamble

I had been meaning to do the Harrow parkrun since practically the beginning of this challenge. I used to live very close to Harrow Park, and ran plenty of circuits of the course while a resident, so I already knew it well. I think the Harrow parkrun actually started shortly before I left in June 2015. I knew it would be a fairly straightforward run around the perimeter with some elevation involved, but nothing that should affect my pace too much. I was also hoping that I might be able to get a PB on this course, given that it was nowhere near as hilly as Hilly Fields, and my cold had improved since last week.
I'd had an early night, but it hadn't done much good as I finally drifted off to sleep some time before 1am, but I felt better than I'd expected when the alarm went off at 6.15am. It was very cold again this week, but I silenced the alarm, got breakfast organised, then got dressed, finally leaving the house (yep, later than expected) at about 7.20am, to run the mile or so to North Ealing station where I pretty much jumped straight on a Piccadilly Line train to Rayner's Lane. At Rayner's Lane I changed to a Metropolitan Line train, listening to music rather than reading my Kindle as this had made me drowsy on previous parkruns. I got off at West Harrow, jogged to the Pinner Road then turned right and continued on to Harrow Cemetery where I ran to the entrance to Harrow Park.
The park was looking gloriously autumnal. There were quite a few dog-walkers but I couldn't see any runners yet, maybe because it wasn't even 8.30am, so I continued my warm up by running around part of the park and re-familiarising myself with the uphill section just so I knew what gradient to expect. When the time drew closer to 9am I headed back down the park to the cricket clubhouse and took off my gillet and track pants. It had been tempting to hold on to them as it was still very chilly, but I didn't want my run to be hampered by too many layers. It was then

time for an up-beat and humorous brief from the run director and then time to walk to the start, not far away on the perimeter path.

The Course

We were counted down from three and let loose. I was in a comfortable position relatively near the front but not too far forward, and was able to get to the pace I wanted without any obstruction, and without obstructing anyone else. The course begins on the lower south-east side of the park and goes in an anti-clockwise direction around the perimeter for three laps. The first lap, however, has an addition. After turning left by a small pavilion, and passing the car park and playground, we turned right, then left by the toilets to follow a small loop around the bowling green that brought us back to the playground where we turned left and passed the toilets again to follow the longer section of the east side of the park which goes uphill (but not severely) to the north end. The small loop was very well designed. When we came back to the path all the other runners seemed to be behind us so there was no chance of collision. The marshal then coned off the diversion to ensure no one was tempted to do it again on the subsequent laps.

At the top of the park we turned left and started to go downhill. When I used to run around Harrow Park I always loved this section. You finish the uphill and know that you've got a short downhill followed by an even longer downhill as a reward. The first, shorter downhill section, along the north side of the park, passes the north exit and a small outdoor gym area, before turning left to then follow the fairly straight west section back down toward the south end of the park, passing the tennis courts and bowling green on the left and the cemetery on the right.

Also on the left as we approached the south end were a series of fallen trees, cut into sections that seemed to form a display. I remembered this tree, or trees falling down in a bad storm some years ago. It was interesting to see them still there and still a part of the park.

At the end of this section of path which circles the cricket pitch there was a left turn, taking us past the cricket nets, then the south exit to Pinner Road, and past the finish funnel with the run director and marshals giving loud encouragement. At the end of this stretch we turned left again and came back to the start line.

Earlier on, while running to North Ealing station from home my whole body had been stiff and my legs had taken a while to get going. For the actual run I felt a lot better, and I put this down to adequate warming up, especially important when the weather is this cold. I managed to pretty much hold on to the fast pace of the first lap, not quite managing a sprint finish but still finishing strong. I took off the thigh support shortly before the run began, thinking it would hamper me too much, and I think it was the right thing to do. I even managed another five miles, running back home to Ealing without it, so the thigh is definitely getting better.

Position: 20 out of 138
Time: 22 minutes 29 seconds.

No PB again, and I still haven't got below twenty-two minutes, but I'll get there. The important thing is that although (perhaps even because) I knew the park so well, I really enjoyed Harrow parkrun and will definitely try to get back there some time. The runners and marshals are very friendly, committed and organised, and the course is straightforward but with that slight twist in the first lap that I thought was quite neat. And the park looked fantastic in its various autumnal colours.

## 19. Crystal Palace
12th November, 2016
'Splash!'


Preamble

I was actually glad that I still had a cold this week, as it made me more drowsy than usual and more inclined to go to bed early on Friday night. The large measure of Night Nurse didn't hurt either. And although I was still less than enthusiastic when the alarm went off at 6.15am, I knew I could be feeling a lot worse (although at this point I was still blissfully unaware of the wet conditions outside).
I made myself a coffee and downed a smoothie (very healthy), followed by strawberry Pop Tarts (not quite so healthy), before dressing in several layers of clothing to brave the cold weather. When I opened the front door I found that while it wasn't quite as cold as I'd expected, it was certainly a lot less dry, so I seethed back up to the flat to retrieve the rain jacket I use for running which, I realised only today, doesn't so much resist the rain as have a discussion with it, and not a particularly heated one. In other words I could have left it behind and I wouldn't have ended up much wetter. Anyway, I was now running late, as usual, so I hot-footed it down the road to Ealing Broadway, managing to catch the desired District Line train to Victoria, where I had minutes to catch the overland train towards London Bridge. I read my Kindle and again I started to feel sleepy, but there wasn't much that could be done about that. I'd shrug that off during the warm up, and while getting soggy.
I was almost falling asleep when the train pulled in at Crystal Palace, but I roused myself and left the station to find a very colourful, if very wet, park. I jogged around the side of the stadium and (having checked my phone outside the station) toward the meeting point for the run. There were a couple of people standing under trees or by the small buildings looking cold and wet but determined, and I wondered if the run would be rained off, but as the clock hands spun around toward nine, more and more hardy folk arrived, unwilling to miss their Saturday parkrun fix for the sake of 'a bit of water.' I did some stretching and jogging and was

ready for the off. After a small brief we assembled slightly further down the path and then got going.

The Course

The course begins on a long, straight, slightly uphill path near Thicket Road, and near the toilet block. On this occasion there was an interesting water feature (a puddle) which changed during the run, to a pond, then a lake (some exaggeration here, maybe), and it did make me think it was a shame that parkruns don't have these as a matter of course. Being used to writing risk assessments myself though, I know that 'hazards' on a parkrun course are never going to be a good idea, no matter how much fun they might be. Shame, but then that's what obstacle courses are for. At the top of the path, not far from the steps up to the leisure college, the course turns right and follows a slightly winding path toward the memorial bell, and the spot where the finish funnel is setup (which you pass through after completing two and a bit laps). The path then turns left where it joins the perimeter path, then right up a short incline, and left again, all on a wide tarmac path, curving around to the right, then opening out on a fairly long path with a view toward the Eiffel Tower-like broadcasting transmitter ahead. There were at least two dogs (with their owners) running today, both very well-behaved and clearly keen parkrunners. Here I was passed by one of the dogs with its owner.

After following the side of the Crystal Palace Concert Bowl the course takes a right, goes dead straight for a while then shortly afterwards curves right again and follows a more or less straight path between trees for some time before turning right, meeting the short incline it followed earlier, and turning left and following the perimeter path all the way back to the start of the run where it was time for lap two. I noticed here that the puddle had grown considerably, and was so busy noticing this that I forgot to detour around it and splashed straight through, soaking my running shoes and socks. Clever. The less said about the state of the 'puddle' the third time through the better, but I still like the idea of a water hazard on the route.

The second lap was a little easier since I didn't have to worry about filming with the GoPro (which I had to keep wiping rain off), and although the clothes I was wearing (particularly the jacket) were a bit restrictive (as well as practically useless), they didn't affect my pace too much. That being said there was no way of a PB this week, so it was a good thing I wasn't banking on one.

Every week I think the same thing: if this were my local parkrun I would be very happy indeed. The rain is a nuisance, sure, but it doesn't spoil what is unarguably a fantastic park and an excellent course. If you live locally, or have been thinking about doing a bit of parkrun tourism, pay Crystal Palace a visit. I doubt many other parks have dinosaurs.

Position: 42 out of 132
Time: 23 minutes 41 seconds.

On paper that's a lot slower than last week, but considering the conditions I don't think it's a bad time for me. And it was a good warm up for the Grand Union Canal Half Marathon the next day.

## 20. Beckenham Place Park
19th November, 2016
'Best served cold'


Preamble

Last week I had my first properly wet parkrun at Crystal Palace, and now it was time for my first properly frosty one. Though despite the cold, and thanks to a clear sky, this actually meant that Beckenham Place's inaugural parkrun was a very brisk but enjoyable one. In order to ensure I had plenty of time for travel delays, I had to get up at 5.45am which was hard, but not as hard as I had expected. One worry, however, was that both my fleece and gillet were both in the washing basket, so I had to make do with a base layer, my parkrun t-shirt over that, then a long sleeve running top on top of that. Three layers should mean I was warm enough, though as I left the flat (on time for once) I still felt that I should have been wearing more. Thankfully a one-mile warm up run to Ealing Broadway did just that –warmed me up, and by the time I got there and boarded the Central Line train to Oxford Circus, the cruel, early morning bite was no longer a concern. Thanks to a good, strong coffee I didn't feel drowsy on the train this week so I was able to read all the way to Victoria where I caught the train I needed to Bromley South with a few minutes to spare. Unsurprisingly for this time on a Saturday morning there were few people around, and hardly anyone on the train.
Bromley South was the first stop, so the journey was only around twenty minutes, and I only had to wait five to ten minutes on the platform for the connecting train to Ravensbourne. It was great to see such a clear, blue sky, and I hoped that the sun would warm things up a bit by the start of the run. The journey to Ravensbourne was a short one, and once out on the almost deserted platform I climbed the stairs to the road and tried to work out where to go next. I actually followed the signs for the Capital Ring trail through the woods and nearly went disastrously wrong before turning back and walking back to the station, then following the road down to the bottom of the hill and turning left. From there it's a simple case of following the path around the outside of the field until you get to

the start of the parkrun. It was a good job my time-keeping had been good today, as despite getting lost I still had plenty of time.

Crunching across the frosty grass I dropped my bag near a collection of bikes and took off my track pants. I was intending to take off my third upper layer too, but due to the cold I decided to hang on to it. I really couldn't see myself getting too hot. After a jog along the path and some stretching near the Ravensbourne River, I headed back and joined the eager throng by the start line. A few people were arriving with seconds to spare, and by the time the run director let us go there were nearly two hundred of us, a great crowd for an inaugural event to go with the glorious surroundings.

The Course

The course begins on the path opposite the railway line and on the other side of the river to the Millwall Football Club training ground. You head south down the path toward Ravesbourne Avenue (and back toward the station), but take a right onto the grass before getting there, following the line of cones toward the other side of the field. There is then a long straight section along that side of the field until you get to the trees at the far end where you turn right back toward the path, then left, taking a path through the trees before very soon taking another left around the next field to follow the path along it's west side. You then pass into a smaller grass section where you loop around the trees at the end to come back on yourself and follow the other side of the three sections before returning to the start for the second lap.

Right away I could feel the temperature making it harder to run. I was still able to move fairly fast, about my average pace for a 5k, but I thought I could have run much faster if the weather had been milder. That said, I didn't really feel psyched up for a PB, so was content just to enjoy the course, which I did. I ran the second lap pretty much as fast as the first, maybe a bit faster, and again I knew I could run harder as I finished quite comfortably rather than collapsing in a heaving pile like a lot of runners who genuinely go all out. I need to work a bit more on getting out of my comfort zone at some point, but there's no rush.

I had my barcode scanned, filmed a few people finishing, then decided I had better make a move as there was another long journey back to Ealing. As I turned off the GoPro and headed off to collect my bag I overheard a runner mispronouncing 'inaugural.' At least I think he mispronounced it. It's a tricky word that.

The weather really does affect the parkrun experience, and though it was 'a bit nippy' the autumn sunshine casting shadows on the grass, from the trees and the runners was fantastic. Just watching the video back makes me want to do Beckenham Place parkrun again. What a fantastic way for the weather and environment to compliment a superb inaugural run. There were plenty of marshals present, no doubt to ensure the first run went as smoothly as possible, and everything felt very finely honed and under control.

Position: 62 out of 193
Time: 22 minutes 39 seconds.

I actually thought the time was going to be a lot slower than that, closer to twenty-four minutes in fact, so this was a nice surprise. It's probably naïve to think there might be milder conditions in the next few weeks that might make it easier to get a faster time, so I'm probably going to just have to get used to the cold weather and find a way of running faster in spite of it. But it's good to have a new challenge to keep things interesting.

# 21. Beckton

26th November, 2016
'Small but perfectly formed'

Preamble

It was another cold morning this week, but I think I'm starting to get used to it. I love seeing the frost on the grass and the mist obscuring the city view from the train early in the morning. A few days before the run I'd decided to visit the Decathlon store at Canada Water because I needed (among other things) some more winter running clothes. Because I'd already done Southwark parkrun (the closest one to it) I chose Beckton, as it was only a short journey away.
I was up at 6.15am, the daylight alarm clock waking me steadily so that it wasn't a sudden shock to the system, made coffee, got dressed and got out of the flat relatively on time to run down the road to Ealing Broadway. I bought a coffee from the coffee shop near the station then headed in. A train was about to leave, and although I didn't want to run to get on before the doors closed, the next train wasn't leaving for another ten minutes, so I had no choice but to get on. I ran 9.5 miles home from work on Friday night and had left my bag, including my Kindle, at work, so I had brought along a hardback copy of *Meditations From the Breakdown Lane: Running Across America* by James Shapiro, a fascinating account of his running from San Franciso to New York unaided. This absorbed me all the way to Oxford Circus, where I realised I should have gotten off at Bond Street, so had to backtrack then catch a Jubilee Line train to Canning Town and change to get to Beckton Park station. I haven't travelled on the Docklands Light Railway much, but it's a funny old line. The stations are very close together, but you can sit right at the front or back (where there would normally be a driver) and get a fantastic view.
I crossed the road and consulted my phone to find the way to the start of the parkrun. I worked out the general direction and ran slowly, warming up, before stopping to take some footage with the GoPro. I had only taken one small clip when the camera turned itself off. Odd. I had put it on charge for at least half an hour the night before so it should have been ok.

I turned it on again, started recording, and off it went again. Oh dear. I figured I might be able to get a couple of clips with my phone, then decided to just film it all as usual. It has to be said that the Samsung phone I have isn't ideally suited to this, especially since it's hard to hold on to it at the best of times, but it was worth it to have something to show at the end.

I found the small building at the other end of the park where the start was indicated and soon other runners appeared. I was surprised there wasn't a larger crowd, but then remembered that some parkruns are smaller than others, and that this was probably normal. I did some stretching, took a few more film clips, then it was time for the run director to brief everyone.


The Course

The start line was just around the corner, and without much ado we set off around the course. The route begins by heading down the west side of Beckton District Park along the tree line, before turning left at the end, following the south side, still on grass, before taking a detour through trees and continuing on over the grass toward a path where it turns left, then shortly afterward left again to follow the trees, this time heading roughly north along the east side of the park up to a long, straight path known as the Beckton Corridor. Here you carry on straight until you reach an obvious lamppost which you circle around before heading back the way you came and turning right, this time over a bridge and then bearing left on a path along the north side of the park which returns you to the gathering point where you turn left and meet up with the path not far beyond the start line. The second lap is pretty much identical to the first, except that instead of turning right over the bridge after completing the out-and-back section along the corridor, you continue on along the tree-lined path that intersects the park, and turn right at the end to follow a route marked by cones toward the finish funnel.

Again the cold weather didn't slow me down too much but it did make the effort feel harder. I stayed pretty much at the same speed all the way around, but didn't push myself to run faster than usual. The long run the night before may also have had some bearing on this. I definitely enjoyed the course though. If you are after a PB and want a nice flat course with some significant straight sections, then Beckton is ideal. It might be best to try it in milder weather if you want the best chance at a good time, but whatever the conditions, Beckton is great. The organisers clearly put some thought into the route and it's another course that changes from one lap to the next which I really like. I would definitely return for another run. There were only forty or so runners, but it was cold after all, and I don't blame anyone who stayed in bed. That said, if you had ventured out you wouldn't have regretted it.

While shopping at Decathlon afterwards, I remembered another reason I love running so much. The gear. I picked up some warmer clothes and a new light for running in the dark, something which is definitely going to come in handy, at least for the next few months.

Position: 11 out of 43
Time: 22 minutes 51 seconds.

I could certainly be accused of not really trying, looking at the results of recent weeks, but then I haven't really been focussed on getting a PB. The filming takes priority and tends to affect my pace, and the cold weather is making it tougher. Also, I think the only way I'm going to get faster is via speed training, something that I'm wary of after the thigh injury. But the important thing is just doing the parkruns every week, something which, thankfully, I don't seem to be getting bored of.

## 22. Richmond
3rd December, 2016
'Every parkrun is the best parkrun'


Preamble

I love Richmond Park, but that's not why I think it's one of the best parkruns there is. I think there are a number of reasons. There's the fact that it's one lap, so no repetition. There's the awe-inspiring, deceptive sense of being out in the countryside rather than in the city, and there's the very high likelihood that at some point you'll turn and see deer. Amazingly, considering how big Richmond Park is (it's the biggest park in London), it always seems busy. Probably because it is. And it's not difficult to see why it's so popular. The numbers for today's parkrun are a good indication of how popular the park is, and I saw at least three groups of cyclists training together as I ran around. I would say that out of all the parkruns I have visited so far, Richmond is second only to Bushy. And it's a very, very close second.

There were a couple of surprises with this run. The first was that getting up wasn't the trial by ordeal it had been the previous few weeks, even though I didn't get a lot of sleep the night before. The temperature was milder than last week, so the urge to stay in bed (and it was definitely there) was a little harder to fight off. I had breakfast and managed to organise myself so that I wasn't quite so late leaving the flat as I normally was. I walked and jogged to Ealing Broadway and caught a District Line train to Turnham Green where I changed to get a train to Richmond. I'd forgotten how quickly I could get to Richmond from Ealing, and wished I'd remembered this in the summer as I could have had some really good training runs. Never mind. Out of Richmond tube station I turned left and walked along the high street before heading up Richmond Hill, running a little to get the legs warmed up. On reaching the park I turned left, knowing the start was along the path somewhere but not exactly where, and because I got there relatively early the organisers and crowd hadn't arrived yet, so after going too far along the path I checked the course map on my phone and backtracked to the entrance where I saw people had started to gather.

I took off my fleece and track pants and did some stretching near a bench. One of the volunteers was doing the introduction for first time runners, and I decided to stick around to listen, even though I'd been to the park before and had run two laps of the course during a 10k. After this it was time for the main brief by the run director (who had to stand on a tree stump so everyone could see him due to the large throng that had now gathered), before we all walked along the path to the start, not far from the small pond. A lot of people run the Richmond parkrun, so it's a lot of bodies to have all huddled together on the narrow path. This means that depending on where you are in the crowd at the beginning, it can be a while before you're able to break into a proper stride. Not that I'm blaming this on my eventual time (I could have made up the time if I'd been monitoring my pace etc.) but it is worth bearing in mind if you're aiming to get a PB at Richmond. Don't worry though – the course more than makes up for the slightly slow start, and it's a small price to pay.

The Course

Once the run was underway the crowd began to stretch out and we headed along the path, away from the pond and back toward the main gate, turning left at the road to follow the roadside path along Sawyer's Hill. This is a good, long stretch with a fair amount of downhill and, as planned, I took the opportunity to get a good, fast pace going. As well as the three groups of cyclist I also spotted some young deer off to the left of the path at one point, frolicking about and almost joining the runners on the path. Eventually it was time to leave Sawyer's Hill to turn left up the grassy path that follows another road north until it turns left again not far from the car park and Fife Road. The route now enters a wooded section before it opens out and follows a long up and down section by the tree line before entering the trees again briefly before the stretch back toward the pond, then the finish line near the main entrance.

I felt great for pretty much the whole length of the course. The nice downhill bits at the beginning encouraged me to move fast, while the uphill sections when they came were brief enough that they weren't able to sap my energy, at least not until the last half mile. Although I wasn't monitoring my pace I was sure that I was running fast and felt that I was pushing myself a little more than usual.

Position: 66 out of 360
Time: 22 minutes 49 seconds.

Going by the time, I could have pushed myself more. And I think that's the point – even if you're running faster than normal, if you feel good, you're probably not running fast enough. I should have pushed even harder at the beginning of the run when I was running strong, and saved the hard work and the gritting of teeth to the end. Again, some people were nearly collapsing when they reached the finish line, and even if they finished after me, their approach was probably better than mine. It's all part of the education, however, and something to think about for next time.
Richmond is a fantastic course. It may be second to Bushy Park, but that, after all, is still a huge compliment. One-lap courses in parkrun aren't that common, and they should be treasured, just like the parks themselves.

## 23. Crane Park
10th December, 2016
'A close run thing'


Preamble

Sometimes, even when a plan works out, you can't help but look back on it and think 'that was stupid.' Take today, for example. A month or so back I entered the Osterley Park 10k, and while I should have given parkrun a miss so I could concentrate on the race, I decided, since there would be an hour's gap between the two, that I would run both Osterley parkrun and the 10k. Then, about a week ago I started to wonder if it was possible to fit in a new parkrun (I'd already run Osterley as part of my 47 Parks challenge), then catch a train or bus to Osterley in time for the race. I looked at Bedfont Lakes as it's only a few miles away, but I wasn't confident that the buses and trains would get me from one venue to the other in time. I then looked at Crane Park and although there was a similar problem, I reckoned I could run the 4 miles from there to Osterley in time for the 10k.
This meant that I would be running a fast 5k, followed by a fairly fast four miles, and then a 10k race. It sounds silly to me now as I write this, so why it didn't before the day I've no idea. But that was the plan and I was determined to stick to it, and bar a slight wobble in navigation it all worked out OK. Except for my legs of course, which now feel like jelly.
I woke at 6.15am, made coffee and porridge and got into my running clothes before leaving the flat late (no point breaking a habit) at about 7.20am. I ran down the road to the station for a nice warm up, finding the temperature a lot milder than expected, and caught a District Line train to Richmond, changing at Turnham Green. On emerging from Richmond station I looked out for the H22 bus stop and found it close by, seeing that the next bus would be along in nine minutes. By now it was past 8am and I didn't know how long it would take to get to Crane Park, but I needn't have worried. The journey was quick and uneventful and I got to Crane Park in time. I've only been to Crane Park once before, while running a section of the London Loop, but I recognised some parts of it as I ran

around. I wandered along the path looking for the finish where I needed to leave my bag for a fast getaway (it's a fair distance from the start) and gave up, leaving it with a very helpful marshal instead who carried it to the finish for me. It's very nice when marshals do this.

I was surprised by how many people were lining up at the start as I had expected it to be quite a small parkrun. There was plenty of room though, and everyone was limbering up and chatting away until it was time for the run director briefing.

The Course

As it was now 9am there was no delay in getting moving and soon the crowd was heading north-west along the dirt path to the woods where the course follows a slightly undulating path through the trees by the Crane Park Island Nature Reserve and toward the A314 Hounslow Road where you take a right turn along the pavement for a short stretch before turning right, back into the park along a fairly wide tarmac path through trees and over open ground before heading toward the River Crane and the prominent River Crane Shot Tower. After a left turn and another slightly twisting section of path, you pass the finishing funnel (marked by cones) and head toward the Great Chertsey Road where you take a right turn, then another right turn to follow the dirt path back towards the start before embarking upon the second lap, which is the same as the first except this time you don't have to resist the temptation to run through the finish cones.

I started off quite fast and maintained a pretty good pace, though nothing faster than usual. Mindful of what was to come I couldn't risk pushing myself or I'd have ended up doing the Osterley 10k on my hands and knees. As it turned out my time was ok, and I still had hope that a PB wasn't far off.

Once the run was over there was no time to hang around – I needed to get going if I wanted to get to Osterley Park in time for the start of the 10k. I retrieved my bag and started jogging toward Great Chertsey Road, cursing myself when I realised I'd forgotten to say thank you to the marshal for ferrying my bag from the start to the finish. I checked my phone and when I reached the main road I crossed over, then crossed over again by the roundabout and started following the Great Chertsey Road north. It was a good job I checked my phone again shortly afterwards as I was going in the wrong direction and had to correct myself, losing valuable time. Luckily there were no more navigational blunders, and I ran the four miles to the 10k via Hounslow, then through Isleworth to Osterley Park, finally reaching the gathering place as everyone was doing their warm-ups, and managing to change into the t-shirt I'd pinned my number to earlier and drop off my bag before everyone started moving to the start line. It's a very strange feeling to begin a race that a lot of people there have trained for (possibly the first event of its kind they have ever done), while you are already exhausted from running. I felt more than a little daft. I knew I should have eaten something more than a two-finger Kit-Kat after finishing the parkrun, but there was now no time, so I would have to rely on water alone to fuel me. The first half of the race was hard but manageable, but after the 5k mark I had the strong feeling that at some point I would need to stop and walk to get some energy back in my legs. Incredibly, after continually putting it off, I got to the finish without walking, and was relieved that it was all over. I retrieved my bag, hi-fived one of the marshals (it would have been rude to refuse), then bought a coffee and headed off on the long walk to Osterley Tube station.

There was more walking once I got to South Ealing, at least a mile of it, but I think it actually helped my legs rather than made them worse. I forgot to stretch which will no doubt come back to haunt me later, possibly in the form of cramp (shudder). In all I had run over fifteen miles, when there was really no need. But I didn't injure myself, and it meant I could (if I wanted to) spend the whole of Sunday in a perpendicular position and not feel guilty. Am I glad I did it? Yes. It was a risky plan, but it paid off. I doubt there will be many more occasions when I can do a parkrun and a race in the same morning. Would I recommend the idea to someone else? Probably not.

Position: 22 out of 110
Time: 22 minutes 34 seconds.

I think I probably ran fast enough considering how many more miles I needed to cover. Still, I can't help but think that ever elusive PB is mocking me, and I need to put it in its place. Maybe next week will be the right time. Crane parkrun offers a nice route, a very friendly bunch of people, and has its own landmark – the shot tower. The course is more or less flat and should allow for a PB if you're really going for it. I would happily return.

## 24. Wormwood Scrubs
17th December, 2016
'Mist opportunity'

Preamble

After the lunacy of the previous weekend - running Crane Park parkun then running to Osterley for the 10k, I decided to take it a little easier on myself this week. But only a bit. Although it would have made more sense to do the parkrun and have a lie-in on Sunday, I saw a few weeks ago that Greenwich were holding a 5k and 10k event on Sunday 18th, and the medal had a nice, festive snowman on it, so I couldn't resist. It was my last week at work and after two Christmas parties in a row on the Thursday and Friday I was exhausted and relieved that it was holiday time. But I still had two more early mornings and runs to do. The alarm went off at 7am and I got up and got myself organised. I was originally thinking of running the four miles from home to Wormwood Scrubs, then maybe running back, but in the end this felt way too ambitious. I had the 10k the next day and I was already in need of some recovery, so instead I ran the mile down the road to Ealing Broadway and caught the Central Line to East Acton. When I got there I checked my phone and navigated my way to the park which was only a short jog down the road, and found a very foggy, seemingly deserted recreation area with crows and those green birds (parakeets I think) that seem to be all over West London now, chirping loudly. Due to the low visibility it wasn't until I was close to it that I could see Wormwood Scrubs prison. I could hear a lot of voices from over the wall. I walked past the start line, and headed on to the finish where a small group of keen parkrunners were already gathering.
Even when it was time to wander down to the start line there were only thirty or so runners, so it was possible that the weather had put others off. They were certainly a keen bunch though, and as we gathered by the start it seemed everyone was itching to get on with it. The run director gave the expected notices and words of encouragement and we were off.

The Course

The course starts halfway along the park's south side, parallel to the prison and heads toward the Linford Christie stadium, taking a left before it gets there and heading north across the grass toward the opposite end of the park, passing a small copse of trees on the way, before turning left and following the long path heading west. This section soon becomes quite muddy and I had to slow down to avoid slipping, wishing I was wearing off-road shoes which some of the other runners clearly were. One guy in fact wasn't wearing shoes at all, running barefoot. He finished just ahead of me so he was obviously on to something. Eventually the muddy section ended, and the course curved around to the left before taking a sharper left, following a long, curving path along the west side of the park before taking another sharp left by the prison, returning to the start line to embark upon the second lap. Despite the slowing down caused by the muddy section I had been running fairly well, and the second lap proceeded much like the first, except that I took a left turn too early before the end of the second lap and started heading back up the park before realising something was wrong, and heading back to the path, seeing other runners catching up. That's the problem with foggy conditions – if there aren't any runners visible ahead of you and you don't know the course very well, you can end up going wrong. Back on track I sped up and soon after completing the second lap I took the correct left turn and was heading toward the finish funnel.
I would say that I enjoyed Wormdwood Scrubs parkrun, despite the muddy section and going wrong. If I was going back I would definitely wear off-road shoes though. There is no hard surface so even if there isn't a lot of mud you can't go wrong with those shoes. Without the fog it would be a much easier course to follow as you'd be able to see people ahead of you even if you fall behind. Still, it does make things interesting, no doubt about that.


Position: 13 out of 34
Time: 24 minutes 04 seconds.

A fairly mediocre result for me, but not surprising considering the slippery, muddy section and the getting lost. If I could only have a nice flat parkrun on tarmac I might be in reach of that fabled PB. That will have to wait until next year though. I will hopefully be running Ludlow parkrun on Christmas Eve. Sounds like a very interesting, if tough, course.

## 25. Brockwell Park
14th January, 2017
'Business as usual'


Preamble

After a three week break from the London parkruns I was really glad to be back at it. After Wormwood Scrubs in December I travelled up to Shropshire to spend Christmas with the family. I knew there were a couple of options for parkruns near them, and sure enough I managed to run Ludlow on Christmas Eve, and Wyre Forest on New Year's Eve with my brother. Like an idiot I forgot my barcode for the Ludlow run, so my performance will be forever recorded as 'unknown,' with a time falling somewhere between 24.29 and 24.51. I had been warned by my brother, Darryl (a far better athlete than me) that it was a technical course with some significant uphill sections and mud in places. I didn't have my off-road shoes with me, but I had bought some snow spikes to put on my road shoes. I tried these out but didn't bother with them in the end as I found them quite uncomfortable to run with. It's not really what they were designed for. Despite its difficulty I did enjoy the Ludlow course and highly recommend it. It follows paths and road through the woodland outside the town and forces you to concentrate a little more on what you're doing.
I went a bit mad with my running over Christmas, doing a 20 mile there-and-back run to Ludlow near the start of the holiday, and a 17 mile run around Clee Hill a few days later, with other long runs added in. This 'overdoing it' led to a problem with my left Achilles tendon, which I'll come to shortly.
On New Year's Eve Darryl and I drove to the Wyre Forest parkrun just outside Bewdley. This was another great wooded course which begins with a short uphill dash from the start, along a woodland path, and then follows a fairly long, progressively downhill section which lulls you into a false sense of security until you remember that what goes down must come up (damned physics!) and are faced with a bit of a climb around the middle and end of the course. I actually did pretty well though, and having

remembered my barcode this time I managed to chalk up a time of 23.28 which, considering the uphill sections and technical nature (i.e. not flat tarmac paths all the way) of the course, was pretty good.

On the Tuesday after returning to London I ran home to Ealing from work in Vauxhall Bridge Road (something I'd started doing before Christmas, a couple of days a week) and found that just as I was finishing my left Achilles tendon was feeling really sore. It was the same the day after too, and I realised that all the extra distance and hill work I'd done over Christmas was now catching up with me. I've been overzealous with my running in the past and paid for it. This meant I now had to rest the foot, at least until it felt ok again. I had a couple of days off running, then on the Friday went for a short evaluation run of around three miles just to see how the foot felt. It was ok, but even strapped up it felt a little sore when I got home, so I made the decision not to do the parkrun the following morning and just keep resting the foot. The following week I did two 5 mile runs in the evening and they were fine. The foot actually seemed to be recovering from the tendonitis quite well. So it looked ok for parkrun the following Saturday, and I chose Brockwell, as it was on paths rather than grass (the weather had been quite wet) and I fancied running to Battersea Park afterwards, then a few miles along the river to Hammersmith to see if both my feet were up for a longer distance again.

Although waking up at 6.15am was no joy, it could have been worse. I had slept ok, despite waking up around 2am with a coughing fit (I had a cold or something), and the weather wasn't as bad as it had been in the week. I had breakfast, dressed and left the flat, catching the bus to Ealing Broadway rather than running there as I was characteristically behind schedule.

I caught a District Line train to Victoria and then jumped straight on an overland train to Herne Hill station, arriving at around 8.15am with plenty of time to spare. I did some warming up, exploring the park, then headed on over to the Lido where everyone was assembling. At about 8.40am there was a fair group gathered, but by 9am there was a throng, an impressive crowd for what I assumed would be a fairly humble parkrun. The run director called everyone together and after the briefing we walked alongside the Lido to the start point. I could see that it would be a slow start with so many people trying to fit on the relatively narrow path, but as the run director had pointed out – the ice on the path needed some negotiating anyway, so the conditions weren't ideal for a PB. I couldn't hear the call to start, but realised we were off when the throng around me started to move. I turned on my music, started my watch and started filming with the GoPro, taking my time and not worrying about my pace as the group was too compact to surge ahead yet anyway.

The Course

From the Lido the course heads northwest, parallel to Dulwich Road, and takes a sharp left when it reaches the west side of the park, shortly afterward heading slightly uphill. This was when it started to open up a little and offer opportunities for overtaking, though because of the muddy grass, care was still needed. It bears right, then takes a left turn, soon passing the lake, before continuing on past Cressingham Gardens and turning left at the end to go downhill along the southern end of the park. After a long stretch adjacent to Norwood Road, the Lido is in view again, and a left turn leads past the finish funnel, then the Lido itself. The first lap went well. My feet felt ok, particularly my right foot (with its long-standing tendon soreness) which despite being painful (for some unknown reason) during the week, was fine for the whole of today's running. The left foot was a little sore, but it too had been strapped up and wasn't a problem.

The pack had spread out by the time I embarked on the second lap, which is almost identical to the first except that it turns left at the end of the Lido to pass the BMX track, missing out the first section of the first lap. I was able to move fairly fast (but probably still my average pace) on the second lap, but did feel like I was tiring by the time I reached the finish. I grabbed a barcode, got it scanned, then retrieved my bag for the run through Brixton and on to Battersea, where I followed the river to Hammersmith, finishing with aching feet but a sense of satisfaction after around 13 miles in total (including the parkrun).

Position: 143 out of 407
Time: 23 minutes 52 seconds.

Wow. 407 is an amazing turnout, and easily one of the busiest parkruns I've attended. And while that number does interest me, the 23 minutes 52 seconds doesn't. But I'm not upset by the result. It wasn't a day for PBs, and I haven't been doing any speed training lately. In fact it wouldn't surprise me if I have to wait for the warmer months before I can make any attempts to better my best time of 22 minutes 7 seconds. But there's no rush, and I'm still enjoying getting out there, visiting new parkruns and areas of London I haven't seen before.

## 26. Dulwich
21st January, 2017
'A sub-zero time'


Preamble

This was my first parkrun in sub-freezing temperatures. It was so cold I had to switch my Go-Pro over to my left hand a couple of times because it felt like my right hand was literally freezing (I had the glove off to get a better grip on it) and I needed to blow on it and rub it to get it warm again. But despite the very cold temperature I finally got another PB. It wasn't below 22 minutes which I had been aiming for, but it was very close.
I chose Dulwich Park at random during the week, and was surprised to find (when checking the map) that it was just down the road from Brockwell Park, where I had run the week before. This meant travel would be easy to work out as it was just one stop along from Herne Hill. When checking the course it looked like a flat, simple route on tarmac path, ideal conditions for a PB. As it turns out, Dulwich is one of the best London parkruns for PBs. You only have to look at the stats on the parkrun website to see that.
At work on Friday I felt drained, possibly due to the runs during the week and not getting enough sleep, but managed to get to bed at the not unreasonable time of 10.30pm. Waking at 6am I quickly rose and got some breakfast. It had taken me all week to edit the video from last week's parkrun, and I realised that trying to do it during the week was a waste of time as I didn't have the energy or the inclination to do much of it in the evenings, so I would go back to doing it on the weekend. I had left the video uploading all night, so I posted it on Facebook and Twitter, then got dressed and ready to leave the flat. I started running toward Ealing Broadway, but as an E1 bus was just pulling up I decided it would make sense to grab it and avoid missing my District Line train from Ealing Broadway to Victoria. The train was waiting when I got to Ealing Broadway and left in good time. When I got to Victoria I first got lost, then found my way to the main hall and saw that I had a few minutes before the 7.55am

train to Orpington (the same train I caught last week) left, so I bought a coffee then hopped on board. The journey was brief, and when I left the train at West Dulwich it suddenly felt like the temperature had dropped even more. I left the station, turned right and jogged down the road, checking my phone at one point to make sure I was going in the right direction. I soon reached Dulwich Park, found the toilets, then did some warming up before heading over to the gathering spot (the same place as the finish) where there were already several groups of people. I ditched my track pants and fleece top, even though it felt very wrong given the cold, then wandered over to the pre-run briefing. It was another big crowd, despite the cold, and everyone seemed keen and fired up. We walked around the corner to the start line and were soon off, following the excellent, wide tarmac path around the outside of the park.

The Course

From the start, near the south entrance to the park, the route turns right and heads in an anti-clockwise direction around the perimeter, passing the large, open grass area where groups were warming up for their own runs and playing football, then passing the American Garden before turning left at the park's east side and heading back west, alongside the east then west lawns. It was here that I realised not wearing my gloves had been a bad idea, and I actually started panicking that my right hand might actually freeze. For the second lap I put the camera (which doesn't seem bothered by sub-zero temperatures) in my pocket and ran with clenched fists, believing I'd left my gloves in my bag back at the finish area, whereas they were actually in a zip pocket in my running top all the time. Soon the course turned left, curving around the boating lake before straightening out and heading past the finish line. That was the first lap done, and I could see, via a tablet one of the marshals was holding up, that my time for the first lap was not much over 7 minutes. If I could keep up that pace I knew I'd have a chance of beating my current personal best time of 22 minutes 7 seconds.
The second lap was pretty much the same as the first, and on the third lap I tried a few times to put on a spurt of speed and push ahead, finding that as I approached the finish line I could have sprinted more, and sadly slowed down realising I had forgotten to get the camera out to film the finish. These precious seconds could have meant the difference between being under and over 22 minutes. I grabbed my bag, had a drink, then ran

back down the road to the station where I stood on the platform waiting for the train to Victoria, visibly steaming away and feeling ridiculously hot.

Position: 65 out of 238
Time: 22 minutes 3 seconds.

It wasn't an outstanding performance, but it got me a new PB so I can't be disappointed. It was four seconds better than my previous best parkrun at Barking last year, when the weather had been at least twenty degrees warmer, there had been a lot less people on the course, and I had started near the front. I was amazed I could do this time in such cold conditions. It was maybe a sign that I had gotten used to running in the cold now, or that my fitness was better than ever. Dulwich is a really great course if you're after a fast time. It's flat, the surface is perfect, and it's just generally a nice park with a really keen crowd of runners. I'm tempted to run Peckham Rye next as it's close to Dulwich and Brockwell, or Orpington as I could take the same train again, but I think for the sake of variety I'd better head in another direction . . .

## 27. Bedfont Lakes
28th January, 2017
'As happy as a man standing in a puddle'


Preamble

As late as Friday I was still unsure of which parkrun to do, but I had narrowed it down to Bedfont Lakes, which I had planned to do a month or so ago but ended up doing the neighbouring Crane Park instead, or Burgess because it was relatively close to the Decathlon store in Canada Water and I fancied doing some more running gear shopping. In the end I opted for Bedfont as I felt this was unfinished business and wanted to get it crossed off the list.
Thankfully it wasn't as cold this morning as on previous Saturdays, so getting up was just the right side of impossible. Rather than silencing the alarm and just lying there in danger of falling asleep again, I was up straight away and soon downing coffee and toast. And without too much dithering I was dressed, geared up and out of the house, running the half mile or so down the road to Northfields station where I caught a Piccadilly Line train to Hatton Cross. So far so good, but there was a frustrating wait outside the station for the H26 bus which arrived just in time at about 8.34am. And luckily it didn't hang around so that I got off at the Bedfont Lakes Industrial Estate at about a quarter to 9. Unfortunately I didn't know where to go from there, so it was down to Old Reliable (the phone) and Google Maps to direct me down the road to the entrance to the park. The sky was a disconcerting shade of grey as I ran, and I had to block my first thought of 'that's just typical,' reminding myself that it's hardly ever rained on my parkruns.
With less than ten minutes to spare I turned into the car park from where I could see a large gathering of people waiting for the run to start. I took off my fleece top and track pants and dropped my bag off by the hot dog stand just as the briefing for first time runners was about to begin. I managed to catch most of this before it was time for the main briefing. It turned out that the run had been cancelled the last two weeks as the park had been closed due to bad weather. It just goes to show how important

it is to check the status of a parkrun before you turn up – if I'd have chosen Bedfont last week or the week before I'd have been fuming at myself.

Once the brief was over (including the introduction of several pacers, which was nice to see), the crowd of 150 or so runners huddled together on the path ready to start.

The Course

The route begins by heading up a slight rise along a mildly twisting path along the south side of one of the lakes. Bearing left further on it follows the south side of a larger lake before taking a left turn, then curving around to the right then heading in an easterly direction toward the Bedfont Road car park before taking a fairly sharp right turn back on itself, then taking a long curve around to the right before embarking on a long straight section that brings you back to the small lake behind the gathering point. Here you turn right, past the gathering point and start the second lap.

The first lap had been ok. I could tell very early on that I was unlikely to get a PB as the course was very wet and the ground uneven and muddy in many places. I also needed to have started closer to the front to get a good start. But never mind, as usual I was happy to just enjoy a new course. At one point on the route there was a puddle that was still pretty much iced over, so one of the marshals was stationed there to stand in the middle of the path and keep people away. He seemed happy enough, and this showed that some responsible person had carried out a risk assessment.

The second lap was pretty much the same as the first. I was tiring but still hanging on, and wondering where the additional section would begin that made the second lap bigger than the first. It wasn't until almost back at the gathering area that I saw runners continuing ahead and taking a circuit of the small lake instead of turning right. I followed after them and soon enough the finish funnel was in sight so I hauled my muddy, panting self through it.

Position: 19 out of 150
Time: 23 minutes 08 seconds.

These were not great conditions for a PB, but Bedfont Lakes is a really lovely course that even with mud and water is still great fun to run. The organisers were clearly looking after everyone by checking the course beforehand and marking out the hazards, and there were a lot of volunteers, so many that we were able to have several pacers. I can't recommend Bedfont Lakes enough. I just have to remember to return in the summer when the weather's nicer.

## 28. Hackney Marshes
4th February, 2017
'Five to ten'


Preamble

The 18 miles I ran last Sunday had worn me out more than I had expected, and not only did I not get enough sleep during the week but when I went for a five mile run around the Ealing Half Marathon route on Thursday night my legs felt stiff, aching and unenthusiastic. More miles does seem to require more sleep, at least for me, but despite this I was still looking forward to the Hackney Marshes parkrun, and the 10k race at the Olympic Velopark afterwards.
The alarm went off at 5.40am and I was out of bed before terrible, dark thoughts of going back to sleep could overcome me. I managed to eat, get dressed and get out of the flat by 7.20am to run to Ealing Broadway where I had to catch a Central Line train to Stratford. When I emerged from Stratford station about 45 minutes later I found it was still cold and wet, a light drizzle slowly dampening my clothes as I walked out of the Westfields shopping centre trying to work out which direction to head in to get to Hackney Marshes. Using the map boards on the street I was able to work out which way to go, but I was worried about time. I ran past the Velopark and alongside a busy road before crossing to a road by the river and following another runner to the entrance of the Hackney Marshes Centre.
It was still drizzling as I had a quick look inside the sports centre and on not seeing any parkrun t-shirts realised this couldn't be the gathering place for the parkrun, and that the actual meeting area was by the river where another crowd had congregated. I jogged over, stashed my bag under the table where it could stay dry, and joined the crowd waiting for the signal to go. I had run a fair distance from Stratford station so I was happy I had warmed up enough, but it was still pretty cold, and everyone seemed keen to get going.

The Course

After a short introduction from the run director it was time to go and we all set off along the wide tarmac path that circles the playing fields and pretty much follows the river the whole way. The route begins with the playing field on the left and the river on the right, turning slightly right before bending in a long curve to the left, through the trees until the path opens up with a wide view of the main marsh to the left. The route then follows a path away from the river before joining it again by the Mandeville Street bridge and the Hackney Marshes changing rooms. It then actually runs beside the river on the towpath before reaching the turn-around point, where it's time to head back the way you came.
Although it took a few seconds to get going at the beginning, the pack soon spread out, mainly due to the nice wide path, and everyone was soon able to get into their stride. I was glad of the run from Stratford station as it seemed to have warmed me up nicely, and although I wasn't on peak form and not well-rested before starting the run, my legs actually felt pretty good, and it seemed like the run on Thursday night might actually have helped rather than made things worse. To begin with I was surprised when fast runners started coming toward us from the opposite direction, then I remembered it was an out and back course, and knew at that point that halfway couldn't be far off. It was nice to pass the turnaround on the towpath and know that you'd passed the halfway point and were heading back to the start. As there is a good path all the way around there is enough space for people running in both directions, but you do need to be aware of other members of the public who might be about, so some awareness is necessary. I will say though that despite its name, Hackney Marshes is not a wet parkrun, except when it's raining of course. But because of the path you don't need to worry about it being muddy under foot. There may be one or two small muddy sections, but generally its good old tarmac.
The way back was ok, and although I was hoping the end would turn up sooner than it did, I didn't feel I was slowing down much, and although it didn't feel like I'd set a great time, it felt good enough given the conditions. I also needed to save some energy for the 10k afterwards.

Position: 60 out of 198
Time: 23 minutes 04 seconds.

It's hard to believe there were nearly two hundred people there. It certainly seemed less to me, so maybe the wide paths made the numbers seem smaller, if that makes any sense. I wasn't feeling on top form this week, so I wasn't expecting too much, and even if I had been fighting fit I might have been holding back for the 10k race afterwards. But despite the cold and wet weather I really enjoyed the course and would definitely love to come back and do it again.

I left Hackney Marshes at around 9.30am and ran back to the Velopark to do the 10k. Again the weather made it difficult to enjoy it too much, but I really liked that it was 6 (and a bit) laps of the course, merging with the runners of the 10 mile race. There were a few different distances on offer, though the 10k was the only one I knew I could make in time after doing the parkrun, and I'm not sure 13 laps of the half marathon course would have been very nice. That's a bit too much repetition for me. Runthrough do some great events though, and their medals are terrific. I finished in 25th place out of 90 runners with a time of 49 minutes, 24 seconds.

## 29. Highbury Fields
11th February, 2017
'Catch 22'


Preamble

Last Saturday's parkrun, followed by a 10k race at the Olympic Velopark, had left me with slightly strained muscles (funny that), so I wasn't on best form this week. I'd managed a couple of five mile runs during the week, but didn't feel much like doing more than that. The cold, wet weather was also starting to get to me a bit and I was really wishing spring would come early. The last two parkruns had been damp too, and it looked like this one would be, but luckily it was light snow rather than rain.
The alarm went off at 6.40am and I was out of bed without delay, getting dressed and eating breakfast, reluctant to turn on the TV in case I got carried away watching something and lost track of time. Incredibly enough I actually left the flat on time at 7.25am this week, so wasn't in a rush as I jogged down the road to Ealing Broadway station where I caught a Central Line train to Oxford Circus. I changed to the Victoria Line and got off at Highbury and Islington at about 8.15am, leaving me with plenty of time before the run. I headed off in the wrong direction to begin with, but using a map nearby I was able to redirect myself back down the road and across from the station to Highbury Fields.
The park itself is almost like an oversized square, as it is bordered on its longest sides by townhouses. I could see now that there was a slight incline (on the longest sides) and wondered if this would affect my pace much. I had decided earlier in the week that I was going to seriously try to get under twenty-two minutes this week, but looking at the slope I wondered if this would be achievable. If my legs were better rested I may have been in with a chance, but I decided to just see how the run went. It was snowing very lightly at this point, and part of me wished it would turn to heavy snow, making for a nice wintery run.
I jogged up the east side of the park and turned left further on to do a bit of warming up. I could see some marshals setting up the finish funnel as I passed the finish point, but there weren't many runners there yet. As I

came back to where I started I could feel the going getting a little tougher, and thought the slight slope may turn out to be a challenge after all. I carried on and while on the second warm-up lap I saw more people congregating near the finish funnel so stopped by a bench to take off my fleece and track pants, then drop my bag off in the pile that had started to form by the funnel. I was hanging around and quite possibly daydreaming when I realised there weren't that many people by the finish anymore, and that perhaps they had headed off to the start point. Oops. I checked my watch and saw that it was almost five to nine, so I took off down the road to the start point where, sure enough, everyone had gathered.

This week I was too far back to hear the run director's briefing, but I'm guessing they passed on all the important information and thanked the marshals. Soon the runners ahead of me were starting their watches, edging faster and faster forward and we were off.

The Course

Because the path around the perimeter of the park is quite wide, it is fairly easy to overtake and soon catch up to whatever pace you are used to. I sped up and crept past a few people to stop myself from getting too comfortable. The route is a slanted, reverse capital 'D' shape and it starts at the bottom of the park near the end of Highbury Crescent, not far from the tube station, and heads north-east up Highbury Place until it meets the top of Highbury Crescent where it turns left on a slightly twisting path before then following the long curve of Highbury Crescent all the way down to the bottom again and back onto Highbury Place where you begin your second lap.

I had a similar worry (though not a big one) to when I ran the 10k last week, which was that I might lose track of how many laps I had completed. It's only five laps, but still – if you hadn't researched Highbury Fields beforehand or had missed the pre-run briefing, you might get caught out.

I don't think I really struggled with the pace at any point, but the upward slope of the first part of each lap probably did slow me down a little. I tried shortening my stride on this section and increasing my footfalls, but for some reason this didn't seem to be as effective as on previous runs, so maybe the legs were more tired than I thought. At the end of the fifth lap, you have to run up Highbury Place once more and just after turning left, head through the finish funnel.

Position: 59 out of 227
Time: 22 minutes 29 seconds.

I genuinely thought I had a chance of achieving the fabled (to me at least) sub-22 minute parkrun, but today it wasn't to be. Maybe if the legs had been fully rested and/or the course had been completely flat I might have done it. Maybe. Each week I am reminded of how being a parkrun tourist makes getting a PB that much more difficult. If you run the same course each week you know what to expect and when to speed up and when to hold back. Even if you regularly run a course with a lot of uphill/technical sections, you can still keep increasing your time just by increasing your familiarity with it. But despite the result, my determination was intact.

# 30. Hampstead Heath
25th February, 2017
'A parkrun with a view'


Preamble

I had a feeling Hampstead Heath parkrun wouldn't be a flat course. I've been there before and I could remember it being quite hilly, so although I was prepared to give the ever elusive PB another go, I was also prepared for that to be a bit too optimistic. But as with other hilly parkruns, the ups and downs are there to be enjoyed, and contribute to the character of the run, so I definitely wasn't disappointed.
I missed parkrun altogether the Saturday before, being out of London and, although Ludlow was close by I had already run it (although I did forget my barcode), so I decided to have a Saturday off. I did manage an 18 mile run during my week off, from Tenbury Wells in Shropshire to Ludlow and back again, and my legs needed more rest than I anticipated, as a 5 mile run four days later (Monday), and another the day after made me realise my legs were functioning ok but tired. I decided to skip the planned Thursday run and rest the legs until Saturday. This seemed to work quite well as although they didn't feel perfect they did feel a lot better, and I seemed to have gotten some energy back by getting some (slightly) earlier nights.
Looking at the map on the parkrun website I decided it was about time I did another north London course, and had been meaning to do Hampstead Heath for a while as I remembered the great views from Parliament Hill. I made sure I knew the best way to get there by train and had a look at Google Maps to determine how to get to the meeting point for the run from the station. It's actually not far from Hampstead Heath (Northern Line) station, and only takes a couple of minutes if you're running.
I was up at 6.40am, wishing it wasn't time to get up so soon and not expecting it to be so cold. I had breakfast and got myself ready to leave the flat at slightly later than the planned 7.15am to run down to Ealing Broadway and catch a Central Line train to Tottenham Court Road, then

change to a Northern Line (Edgeware) train to Hampstead Heath. When I reached my destination I saw that there was a lift taking commuters from the platform to street level, and although the nearby sign said to only use the stairs in an emergency, I decided they would be much more fun. The sign also warned there were 320 steps in total, a pretty scary number which only really sunk in once I was halfway up. And while the staircase didn't seem to go on forever, it was certainly a workout. I wouldn't have been surprised to find a skeleton on one of the landings.

Once out of the station I turned left and jogged down the road, looking out for the left turn I needed. I'd actually memorised the route from the station to the parkrun via Google Streetview, a nifty timesaver. I reached the car park on the heath at just before 8.30am so had plenty of time for more of a warmup before everyone started congregating near the finish line. It had been overcast when I woke earlier, and it looked ever greyer now, a stark contrast to the day before when there had been gloriously blue skies. I was seriously pining for Summer now.

By about ten to nine the numbers had boosted from half a dozen early arrivals to close to three hundred keen runners. At the briefing for first-timers there was an impressively large crowd. It's great to see parkrun is still attracting newcomers and tourists alike. After that it was the main briefing, and time for everyone to walk down the hill to the small bridge where the run begins.

The Course

The route begins from the bridge over the bathing pond, heading in a roughly north-east direction to the right and uphill before very soon curving around to the left and following a long section that eventually comes out by the side of a green then turns right uphill onto Lime Avenue. The route goes first uphill through trees, then takes a fairly steep downhill toward the boating pond where it turns right along the pond's edge before heading in the direction of Parliament Hill, eventually turning right (instead of left toward the viewpoint itself) and heading along the south, then west side of the heath before reaching the start of lap two. Lap two is a repeat of the previous loop of the heath, with an extension that takes you back to the bridge where you began, then across it and up the hill to the finish funnel near the car park.

Because of the hills I knew the PB would be off the table again, but I still ran hard, almost hitting the wall on the second lap on the uphill section heading toward the Parliament Hill viewpoint. As I knew the section wasn't too long I was able to push myself on, but there was a horrible moment when I thought I would actually need to stop and walk. That hasn't happened for a while, and just goes to show how fast I was going on the uphill sections.

Position: 48 out of 275
Time: 23 minutes 07 seconds.

I'm actually very happy with the time, and think that if I had been running a flat course this week I may well have got a PB. I really slowed down on the uphill section on the latter part of lap two, but even with that the final time was probably faster than I expected. Hampstead Heath is a terrific course that certainly requires repeat running. I can't wait to come back some time in the Summer for a run and another look at the awesome view from Parliament Hill across the city, one of the best views in the capital along with Ally Pally. Hampstead Heath is (as I have pointed out) a hilly parkrun, so not ideal for a PB unless this is your local parkrun, in which case regular running of the course should help you get to know the ins and outs and master those hills.

## 31. Kingston
4th March, 2017
'Riverside pursuits'


Preamble

I'll say it right away – no PB this week. I was close, very close in fact, but despite some good, solid running and starting the finishing sprint earlier than usual, I was still four seconds away from my long-time goal of a sub-22 minute parkrun. Still, never mind. I had only just started interval training again the week before, so there was no point getting fed up. It would come, I just had to be patient.
Although the Kingston course is nice and flat (being chiefly along the Thames riverside) there were some muddy sections today which did slow me down a bit. It also goes off the main path in the loop that takes you back on yourself (it's an out-and-back course) and this section was a tad slippery too. It was nothing that slowed me down too much, but if it had been entirely on a flat path I may have ended up several seconds better off. I know – moan, moan, moan. It's the run that counts though, not the time. And the Kingston course is an excellent one.
Once again I abstained from alcohol on the Friday night and tried to get a relatively early night, although I did wake up a few times in the night, restless for some reason, and nearly ignored the alarm, taking a lot longer than usual to silence it. But although I was tired, and although the legs were quite stiff when I jogged down the road to the 65 bus stop at Ealing Broadway, they soon perked up once I got to Kingston and had a bit more of a warm up along the river.
I actually got to gathering point of the parkrun, by the YMCA, at around 8.30am, so had plenty of time to wake up the legs and check out the first section of the course. It was nice to see that, despite still being quite chilly, there was blue sky above, something I hadn't seen for a while at parkrun. In fact most of the 2017 parkruns so far had been either drizzly or cold and grey, so at last it looked like things were finally looking up. After my warm up along the river I returned to find a large group now assembled, and we were soon making our way down the towpath to the

start point. The course does require care on the part of the runner as there are plenty of other path users about. The general rule seems to be to keep to the left at all times and allow other runners, walkers and cyclists to pass on your right.

The Course

From the start point on the towpath behind the Hawker centre, the course follows the tarmac riverside cycle path to Teddington lock where it passes under the footbridge and continues on along the towpath past Thames Young Mariners and on along a more uneven, metalled path. It is this stretch, between the trees, where you are most likely to find a lot of mud and puddles after wet weather. At the end of this section you'll find a marshal who directs runners onto a small loop on the Hamlands. This brings you back onto the towpath by Thames Young Mariners. From there you follow the route all the way back to the Hawker centre, with the finish funnel just off the path on the left.

I positioned myself not far from the front and once everyone was running I managed to get forward to join the front runners, though not for very long. Starting at the front does seem to be a key part of getting a PB though – it encourages a fast pace right from the beginning, though obviously it'll come back to bite you if you run out of steam long before the finish, so some fast pace endurance is needed. At one point early on my music skipped to a random track then stopped altogether, and after a bit of fiddling with my ipod I realised I'd dropped back a bit and so cursed myself. I've always thought the benefits of listening to music while running are debatable. Certainly during a 5k run you're not likely to need music to alleviate any monotony, but it does help motivate me quite a bit, at least if the music player isn't in a playful mood. Once I'd sorted the music out I was running at a good, fast (for me at least) pace that hovered around 7 minutes per mile. I knew I had a good chance at a PB, but the mud soon gave me doubts. At the end of the long 'out' section a marshal directed us to the right and onto the loop around Hamlands, a nice, if muddy, section and given that most people seemed to be behind us I was again hopeful of a good time. Joining the towpath again I tried to maintain a solid pace all the way to the finish, and although the finishing sprint was good, I need to start it earlier next time, as uncomfortable and counterintuitive as this feels. 'No pain, no gain' is an overused cliché for a reason.

I really like Kingston parkrun. Any route that follows a river for most of its length has to be a winner. There are other path users and (after bad weather) mud to contend with, but those things can't stop the route from being an excellent use of five kilometres. I can't wait to return.

Position: 21 out of 189
Time: 22 minutes 03 seconds.

This equals my previous PB, so I neither beat my best time or ran slower. It is a little frustrating, but then again, I can't really complain about running my best time ever, particularly when the route wasn't entirely flat, without obstacles or without me messing about with my rebellious music player. The PB can't be far off.

## 32. Oak Hill
18th March, 2017
'Two thirds done'

Preamble

Having achieved my long-standing goal of getting below 22 minutes at Milton Keynes the week before, I wasn't so focussed on getting a PB this week. This was a good thing because my legs really weren't up to it. It's strange because I had two really good training sessions during the week and my legs felt great on Thursday and Friday, better than they'd felt for a long time, but for some reason on Saturday morning they were stiff, aching and just not at all interested in parkrun. It might be down to having only four hours sleep and getting up at 6am for a long train journey up to Arnos Grove, but whatever the reason, I knew I'd have a struggle getting close to the great time of the previous week.

I've always had trouble sleeping when the seasons change and the temperature fluctuates. But somehow I got to sleep at 2am and the next thing I knew it was 5.45am, leaving only fifteen minutes until the alarm went off. I got out of bed straight away to avoid dozing off again and had breakfast, got dressed, then left the flat a record-breaking 18 minutes later than I'd planned, nearly an hour after getting out of bed. This was unbelievable considering I hadn't wasted any time. Anyway, I ran pretty much as soon as I was out the door, passing Ealing Broadway about ten minutes later and pressing on to Ealing Common where I caught a Piccadilly Line train toward Cockfosters. About an hour later, as I was in serious danger of nodding off, the train pulled into Arnos Grove station and I got out, turning left and finding the road that led to Arnos Park where (having checked on Google Maps the day before) I knew I could follow Pymmes Brook all the way to Oak Hill Park.

The legs hadn't perked up at all, despite the earlier warm up run to the station. I walked through the car park, across the footbridge and found the finish funnel where I dropped my bag before jogging along the path for a while, then running back to do some stretches. A few minutes later there was a newcomers' briefing (there was a lot of them), and then everyone walked over the small bridge and down toward the start point for the main briefing. I positioned myself near, but not too near, the front of the crowd and soon we were off.

The Course

The three-lap course is a pretty straightforward loop, with the last lap being slightly shorter and finishing just before the small footbridge by the car park.
The course starts on the path by the pavilion. It heads northwest and crosses Pymmes Brook over a small footbridge, then continues on all the way to the far northwest end of the park where it takes a sharp left turn, almost coming back upon itself by the park information board. Here you can get a good look both at runners ahead of you, and at runners behind you as they head to the corner. There is now another long straight, parallel to Church Hill Road until you get to some trees where you bend slightly to the left and strike out along a path across the main body of the park. Just before the end of this path you break left and soon pass Oak Hill Bowls Club on your left and the finish funnel on your right. You then go over the bridge and turn left to follow the long path (Pymmes Brook Trail) which brings you back alongside the pavilion and onto lap two.
I started strong enough on the first lap and managed to keep up a fairly good pace on the second and third lap, breaking into the usual sprint as I came to the finish, but I knew that my apathetic legs had prevented me from a great performance. It was a shame but not too much of a disappointment given that I'd got a personal best the week before and broken the long-elusive 22 minute barrier.
It was great to see so many junior runners at the front of the pack, showing the adults how it was done. And as at Kingston two weeks ago, there were signs that the good weather was on its way back, as the sun broke through the clouds during the run and actually felt pretty warm. All in all, and despite the sore legs, another great park and run.

Position: 31 out of 178
Time: 22 minutes 22 seconds.

If I'd had a result like this last year when I was starting this challenge I would have been over the moon. I've definitely improved since then, and even though a different course each week makes it hard to keep bettering my times, I'm pretty sure there are more sub-22 minute runs to come. I just need to make sure my legs get the rest they need on the Friday night. I actually went on to run another 8.5 miles, finishing at Finsbury Park where I did a lap of that parkrun course. It just goes to show that even if the legs aren't up to it, you can still make them work against their will.

## 33. Wanstead Flats
25th March, 2017
'Another five to ten'

Preamble

If there was ever proof of how much difference the weather can make to a run, today was it. The forecast promised glorious sunshine and that's exactly what was delivered. It did come with a side order of blustery, chill wind, but that probably helped everyone stay cool. The other great thing about today's run was that I beat my best time again, only two weeks after the last time, with another sub-22 minute run.
I had signed up to do the Runthrough 10k event at the Velopark in Stratford, and as I'd already run Hackney Marshes parkrun, which is close to the Velopark, I had to find another venue that I could run and have enough time to get to the 10k afterwards (it started at 10.15am). I soon realised Wanstead Flats was my best option, only being a couple of miles away, and although I could have used public transport to get from one to the other, I ended up getting there via a mix of walking and running.
I managed to get a good night's sleep this week, something I was determined to do after last week, when four hours sleep left me with aching legs and a harder than usual parkrun at Oak Hill. I was out of bed with the alarm, almost with a spring in my step and through some miracle managed to leave the flat on time, jogging comfortably down to Ealing Broadway where I caught a Central Line train that took me all the way to Leytonstone. Leaving the train at about 8.15am I walked out of the station and checked my phone to find the best way to get to Wanstead Flats. Straight away I saw I had taken the wrong exit (good start), so I backtracked and left the station via the other exit onto Church Lane, turning right onto the high road and following it all the way to Ferndale Road which led to the flats.
I headed onto the green and could again see what an amazing morning it had become. When I'd left home earlier it was quite cold, but as expected it had warmed up a little, despite the strong breeze. I headed along the outside of the green to the pavilion where a few runners had already arrived and were warming up and chatting. I did some more jogging and

stretching, not wanting to do too much damage to my legs given I had to tackle a race afterwards. I was also wondering if I should be pushing myself on the parkrun too, since going all out surely wasn't likely to lead to a comfortable 10k. I decided to just see how it went.

Once everyone had congregated, the Run Director gave his briefing and we walked away from the pavilion and a short way around the green to the start point. I had positioned myself quite near the front, and although it wasn't a mistake, I did wonder if I was maybe misjudging things. I also started off too quickly, but managed to even out my pace soon afterwards, avoiding burnout.

The Course

From the south side of the park the course heads west for a very short distance toward the two imposing apartment blocks before taking a right turn and heading north along the park's west perimeter for a stretch before turning north-east between a long avenue of trees on a flat dirt track. This is the longest straight section of the route, and probably the best section for picking up some speed or regaining lost ground. Toward the end of the straight the trees are denser and it appears as though you are entering woodland. This is the beginning of a lovely section that begins by turning north-west off the straight and into the trees, soon heading uphill slightly before turning right near the Quaker meeting house and curving around and back onto the straight at its furthest end, heading back on itself. It's here that the runners who are behind you on the lap will be running toward you before turning into the trees themselves. The main straight is followed again for about a third of its length before taking a turnoff on the left, heading south now on another long straight between trees, all the way to the bottom of the park where you eventually turn right and around the main green, back toward the start, passing the finish funnel on the way.

I knew the first lap had been a strong one. Starting near the front of the group and running fast for a while before slowing slightly had actually paid off, and going into the second lap I found I had more than enough energy to keep me going and avoid slowing down further. The weather probably helped too, more for morale than anything else. It certainly helped that the course was mainly flat and not too technical, with a couple of long, simple straights and running on soft grass. As I headed onto the green for the second time I increased my pace, knowing the finishing funnel was in sight, and also knowing that I couldn't be too far off the personal best time I set in Milton Keynes two weeks ago.

Position: 21 out of 167
Time: 21 minutes 50 seconds.

I certainly didn't have my heart set on a personal best time this week, but that doesn't mean it wasn't appreciated. I really enjoyed Wanstead Flats. The weather certainly helped, but even without the sunshine there is a great course with some great sections and surfaces - perfect if you want a crack at getting a personal best time. Almost as soon as I was finished I grabbed my bag and headed off toward the 10k at the Velopark. Although I had a straight road to follow all the way there my legs were aching and stiff, so I knew if I had any hope of getting through the 10k I'd need to do some stretching beforehand. Luckily I got there in plenty of time to get the legs prepared for round two. As with Hackney Marshes I wouldn't recommend doing two events like this in the same morning, or even in the same day, but not wanting to miss either I decided to take the risk. Hopefully the legs will be better for it . . .

## 34. Harrow Lodge
1st April, 2017
'No fools here'

Preamble

I chose Harrow Lodge this week for two reasons: the first was because I thought that a one lap course would make it easier for me to PB again, and the second was because it was the most easterly Greater London parkrun left on the list and I wanted to work my way inwards with the parkruns that were left. I finished the run pretty close to my best time, as it turned out, but something was obviously not quite right this week. The parkrun and 10k race double bill last Saturday had definitely took it out of my legs. I managed a nine mile run on Tuesday night but the legs were sluggish, and though I tried several times to run at race pace, they just weren't having it. Because of this I didn't run for the rest of the week, guessing my legs needed more rest, and I think I was right. Although I wasn't at my fastest at Harrow Lodge, the legs were certainly interested in running fast again.
When first looking at the list of Greater London parkruns I made the same mistake a lot of people must make, in thinking that Harrow Lodge Park must be somewhere in or near Harrow. It isn't. While Harrow is in northwest London, Harrow Lodge Park is on the eastern fringe near Romford, Upminster and the M25. I wonder how many runners have turned up at Harrow parkrun looking for their friends, only to find out later that their friends were looking for them on the other side of London. Still, so long as you do your research beforehand (which you should) there's no real excuse to come unstuck, and it's hardly the only case of place names turning up where you'd least expect them to.
I slept ok Friday night and was almost awake by the time the alarm went off at 6am, so that it wasn't too big a deal rousing myself and getting out of bed. It was still dark outside when I went to the window, and there were ominous clouds above, but although it did speck with rain on the way to the station, the bad weather held off, and the sunny spells came as promised later on.

I had breakfast of coffee, smoothie and a cereal drink (experimenting with an all-liquid breakfast this week), got dressed and then jogged down to Ealing Broadway just as the train I should have caught was pulling away. This left a second Central Line train which was scheduled to leave in thirteen minutes time. The plan had been to catch a Central Line train to Mile End and then switch to the District Line for the remainder of the journey to Elm Park (the closest tube station to Harrow Lodge). There was a District Line train on the platform opposite, and it looked like it was close to leaving, so I got on board that instead. It would take me all the way to Elm Park without having to change, but the journey would be slower. I figured that as I would have to wait thirteen minutes for the Central Line train anyway, there probably wasn't much difference.

Leaving Ealing at about 7am it took the train around an hour and twenty minutes to get to my destination, about ten minutes or so sooner than I had expected, meaning I had plenty of time. I checked my phone to find the direction of the park and headed off down St Nicholas Avenue, finding the entrance to the park at the end. Checking my phone again I saw that the start/finish point was to my right, so I warmed up by running down to the car park where people had started to gather. I still had to find the toilets though, which after some difficulty and re-checking of my phone I realised were in the leisure centre. Once I'd seen to that I headed off back to the car park to find a lot more people had turned up and were warming up and stretching.

I dropped my bag and joined the others to walk the very short distance to the start. As it was April Fool's day it had been decided to run the course in reverse, something that isn't done very often, apparently. Not that it made much difference to me as I had never run it either way.

The Course

Once we'd been counted down we left the start and rushed off across the grass toward the west end of the lake, following the path around it and along its north side, where you get a great view of the runners behind you, until the path took us to the bottom, south end of the park where we then turned and headed northeast. I had started off pretty fast and managed to keep up a good pace, but as I reached the leisure centre and started the circuit around the small sports field behind it, I saw the 2km marker and realised I hadn't run quite as far as I had thought. But I wasn't prepared to let this get me down and pushed on, around the perimeter of the field and alongside the leisure centre car park toward a path where a marshal directed me to turn right toward the north perimeter path. The course now headed southwest back toward the lake, but instead of rejoining that path it took a wider loop, curving around and nearly hitting the western edge of the park, before turning around a tree and heading more or less straight back to the start/finish point. At the tree I heard a marshal warn not to go too fast as there was still a way to go, and thankfully I listened to him, as I really would have been a fool if I'd started a finishing sprint that early. After a few more minutes of puffing and panting in the sun I headed towards and through the finish funnel, this time remembering to stop my watch, which must have been a first.

Position: 12 out of 143
Time: 22 minutes 20 seconds.

I wasn't hoping for a PB this week, although I was surprised to find I was thirty seconds off my current best time. I'm not sure why that is. It might be that my legs were still recovering after the surprise torture I inflicted on them last week, or it could be that the course was a little more technical than I had expected (there is a lot of off-path running). Either way it was a decent time and I am happy with it.
Harrow Lodge is a nice park and appears to be put to full use as there were a couple of groups taking part in some sport or other while parkrun was in operation. As for the course, I really liked it. It has just the right mix of on and off path running with enough changing of scenery to keep you interested and a little bit of up and down, but not too much. Would definitely come back.

## 35. Roundshaw Downs
8th April, 2017
'Here comes the sun'


Preamble

A couple of weeks ago I'd crossed off Oak Hill, the northernmost Greater London parkrun (from the ones left on my list), and last week Harrow Lodge, the most Easterly one. This week I wanted to cross off the most southerly parkrun left to visit, which was Roundshaw Downs. Looking at videos of it on youtube it seemed to be a nice, flat course on grass, and with the weather expected to be good I was really looking forward to it.
Annoyingly, I was engrossed in a pretty interesting (if predictably surreal) dream when the alarm went off at 6am, so after some sighing and remembering who I was and what day it was, I got up, ate breakfast and got dressed. I was trying out a pair of shorts with a sewn in compression layer that I'd bought from Decathlon in Canada Water earlier in the week. I'd only gone to look at compression but ended up like a kid in a sweet shop, buying quite a lot of nice things that arguably I did need but probably still shouldn't have spent so much money on. Anyway, the shorts seemed like a great design so parkrun was the ideal opportunity to test them out and see if the compression was up to scratch, which it seemed to be. I left the flat wearing the shorts and a t-shirt and long-sleeve t-shirt, and I was surprised at how cold it was. I thought for a moment that going back and putting on more clothes might be a good idea, but in the end decided to brave it, after all the forecast had promised it would warm up. I walked rather than ran to the station this time and caught an earlier District Line train than the one I needed, getting to Victoria station in plenty of time for the 7.53 to East Grinstead.
The morning was getting brighter as the train headed out of Victoria and across the river toward South London. In about twenty minutes it pulled into Sanderstead and I got off and left the station, taking out my phone to work out which direction to head in. It wasn't a straightforward route to Roundshaw Downs from Sanderstead station, and there are closer stations, but I chose this one as it meant the least complicated and

shortest journey from Ealing. I headed off, checking my phone every few minutes and soon came to the Purley Way playing fields. I wasn't sure if it was possible to just cut across (it is) as I couldn't see the other side, so I ran around instead and after running up the busy A23 soon came to the war memorial at the edge of Roundshaw Open Space.

There were a handful of people by the finish area, so I headed over, dropped my bag and did some stretching until it was time for the run director to lead everyone to the start point just over the small rise. The sky was completely cloudless, but it wasn't too hot, in fact it was absolutely ideal. There were a few first time parkrunners, as well as visitors, including one from Cardiff, and after the usual notices and information for first time runners the run got underway.

The start of the course is not far from Imperial Way and the large Costco wholesaler. You begin by heading west, straight across the grass toward a long line of trees that you follow almost to the end before curving around to the left and heading south toward more trees, following them until you turn left again and east, before running around and through a small cluster of trees from which you emerge onto grass again, up a hill, through a gate, then further up the hill in a southerly direction before turning left at the southern edge of the downs and left again soon after to head back to the finish point. It's a long, straight run to the finish funnel from here so, as with Harrow Lodge last week, I made a mental note not to sprint too early at the end of the second lap. I passed the finish funnel and the small group of marshals and well-wishers, and carried on to begin the second lap.

I had started fairly fast, though I felt I could have gone out faster, but I wasn't too fussed about getting a great time, and I could always make up time on the second lap if I wanted to. As the crowd spread out over the two laps I had more room to alter my pace if needed and managed to maintain a good enough pace for the whole run without burning out. There were also a few other runners who had a similar pace, so I was able to stick with them for a while to ensure I wasn't slowing down too much. When I reached the end of the second lap I sped up and sprinted to the finish funnel, thankful that the sun hadn't been hotter as I was hot enough. Once I'd got my barcode and token scanned I grabbed my bag and headed back to the station, remembering most of the route without needing my phone.

When I arrived back at Victoria station on the way home, I saw a guy wearing a medal from the Runthrough race at Battersea Park. I guessed it was this event – the medal seemed to be in the shape of Battersea power station. It reminded me that I'd signed up to do the Runthrough 10k at Greenwich the next day. That meant no lie-in at all this weekend, which was annoying, but at least it was made up for with an excellent parkrun and a, no doubt, great race on the Sunday. Once back in Ealing and having done some shopping I headed straight back out to do a couple of laps of the parks nearby. It must have been the weather but for some reason all I wanted to do was run.

Position: 18 out of 150
Time: 21 minutes 51 seconds.

I was genuinely surprised to find I'd got another sub-22 minute time. It didn't feel like I'd run hard enough to do it, so I was obviously fitter than I thought. I could have run faster too, so it will be interesting to see what time I would get on an all-flat, tarmac path course now. Saying that, you can't really beat a course like Roundshaw Downs – lots of flat, soft grass and trail, plenty of turns and some ups and downs. And the weather . . . It couldn't have been better. Great course and a friendly bunch.

# 36. Orpington
22nd April, 2017
'Achilles'


Preamble

Last night I set the alarm for 6am to give myself plenty of time to get from Ealing to Orpington, and I was deep in dreamland when it went off. I was determined to leave on time this week, so got dressed and fed with no hanging around, noticing when I opened the curtains that it looked like it was going to be a bright, sunny day. It actually got less bright and sunny as the morning wore on, but at least it didn't rain. I left the house at 6.30am to walk and jog down to Ealing Broadway where I caught a Central Line train that was just about to leave.
I reached Victoria Station at about 7.25am, leaving me plenty of time before the 7.55am train I'd planned to catch, and was actually able to catch the earlier 7.40am train. The journey South from Victoria is one I had taken before to visit other parkruns, and to hike a section of the London Outer Orbital Path (LOOP), but this was the first time I'd gone to the end of the line. Very few people got off the train at Orpington when it reached there at about 8.20am. I left the station and walked down to the main road, turning left to find Tower Road which I remembered from checking the map while on the train. This soon led to The Avenue and then Park Avenue where I found Goddington Park. I followed a footpath leading in to the park and soon saw a volunteer attaching a warning sign to one of the bollards on the path. Emerging into the wide open expanse of the park I could see some fluorescent jackets on the opposite side and what looked like the finish funnel so I knew I was in the right place.
I had run most of the way from the station and jogged a little more now but I had a problem. The week before I had run Ludlow parkrun, one of the hilliest I've run so far, and on top of that had run an additional (and ill-advised) 9 miles of a route that also had its fair share of hills, a day's activity that resulted in a very sore right Achilles tendon. I had taken it easy in the week between but had still managed a couple of short runs, and a 9 mile walk on the Friday, so I hadn't exactly let the tendon rest. It

wasn't in the best condition for a parkrun, but I didn't want to miss a week, so I decided that if necessary I would amble around the course at a slow pace and just take it easy. There was no need to go mad and risk injury.

Reaching the finish area I dropped my bag and did some stretches, seeing a steady stream of runners arrive from all directions. My heel didn't feel as bad as I had expected, and although I knew I had no chance of getting close to my personal best time, I thought I might still be able to keep a good pace.

The Run Director called for anyone new to Orpington to huddle around him so I went over. He outlined the course route including the extension around the rugby pitch and then it was time for the main briefing. It was good to see several dogs with their owners there, including one who was particularly animated and sounded like it wanted to give the run briefing itself. A second run director reminded the crowd that everyone was welcome at parkrun and to give other runners plenty of room on the course. He also stressed (importantly) that parkrun was a run and not a race. It was a very decent-sized crowd and after the countdown everyone set off toward the first corner, amid the sound of watches being started, friendly chatter and the odd bark or two.


The Course

From the start, near the pavilion, the course heads initially forward before very soon turning right and heading up the park along the line of markers before heading diagonally right when it reaches the playground, towards some trees. It then turns around a corner to the left before joining a tree-lined path that bends slightly left at one point before reaching a perimeter path. It is the tree-lined path where you will encounter the concrete bollards. They do have the very obvious warning signs attached to them, but you should still be prepared as there may be other runners obstructing your view until the last moment. Once on the perimeter path you follow it as it curves and winds slightly downhill before you leave it, cross the grass and join another path along the outside of the park, this one characterized by its slightly uphill gradient and the many tree roots that riddle the ground. At the end of this section of path you turn right onto a similar path, then are soon out in the open again and heading towards the finish funnel. Before the finish and the cheering volunteers however, you must turn left into the rugby field and run around the outside, following the cones until you re-join the main park next to the pavilion. It is now time for lap 2 which is the same as lap 1, and following that, a third lap which is the same as the previous two laps except that instead of entering the rugby field for a third time you head straight to and through the finish funnel.

I ran comfortably for the first lap, careful not to over-extend myself and turn a sore foot into an injured one, but during the second and third laps, when I realised I wasn't in as much danger of injury as I thought, I was able to up the pace and push myself a lot more. There was definitely some favouring and compensation going on however, as the legs weren't moving as fast as I wanted them to, and I couldn't reach my usual pace. Nevertheless I ran a lot stronger than I had expected and was very happy with the result.

Position: 26 out of 183
Time: 22 minutes 39 seconds.

The Orpington course is another winner. When I run a course I'm unfamiliar with (which is basically every week), I find the multiple lap courses give you a chance to properly assess them and work out (during the first lap) what you need to do to best handle the subsequent laps. Although I love one-lap courses because they have more variety and no repetition, I can tend to struggle sometimes (unless I'm constantly looking at my watch) to work out if I'm going too fast or too slow. Some courses with multiple laps can get boring, even if you haven't run them before, but thankfully Orpington isn't one of those. There is enough variety in the lap itself to make it interesting, and you need to have your wits about you to avoid those bollards and tree routes. It's definitely worth another visit.

## 37. Burgess Park
29th April, 2017
'Fast times'


Preamble

The most startling thing today, aside from my time, which I'll come to in a bit, was the weather. When I left the flat it was almost freezing, but just after finishing today's parkrun I thought I would melt. It was so hot. Oddly enough the weather then got colder again, but maybe it's not so odd considering which country we're in and the time of year (but mainly which country we're in).
Earlier in the week I had chosen Burgess Park for this week's run, partly because it was one of the last 11 Greater London parks left in my 47 Parks challenge but also because I wanted to visit the Decathlon store in Surrey Quays again for a spot of shopping. It also meant I could revisit Southwark Park on the way.
I didn't sleep too great the night before but I was still out of bed seconds after the alarm went off at 6.15am. The only possible reason for this is that my body and brain are used to it. Saturday lie-ins, sadly, have now become a thing of the past. I had a good breakfast and sorted my kit out, leaving the house slightly earlier than planned at 6.55am to walk and jog to Ealing Broadway. I was wearing three top layers and shorts with track pants over them, which felt comfortable but if I'd kept all this on for the run I'd have probably collapsed from heat exhaustion.
At the station I caught a waiting Central Line train to Tottenham Court Road, then a Northern Line train to Kennington. I had planned to go to Oval station but all the trains on the board had been for Kennington, so I took a chance that it wouldn't mean much additional distance to Burgess Park as the two stations were next to each other on the map. I still had to refer to my phone to guide me to Burgess Park, which actually turned out to be a lot closer than I had expected.
Once I reached the park I found the start point, but being nearly forty minutes early I took the opportunity to have a run around, warm up and get an idea of the size of the place, which, as parks go, is considerable.

There was a long line of trailers lined up along one side of the park, that were obviously part of filming for a movie or TV series, but not a lot of activity. I stopped on top of a hill not far from the lake to remove some layers and do some stretches. By now the clouds had cleared nicely and it was starting to get very warm. I did some more running and noticed more and more people heading toward the other side of the park so I followed them to the finish funnel and dropped my bag off. It was soon time to head to the start and a lot of people had congregated, including a fair number of first timers to Burgess who huddled around one of the volunteers for a thorough pre-run briefing to go through the course, which would be tricky to remember if you hadn't had an induction or were so fast there was no one in front of you to follow. Then came time for a few words from the Run Director, followed by the countdown.

The Course

From the tennis courts at the Walworth Road end of the park, the course heads dead straight for practically the whole length of the park, and is quite possibly the longest straight I've run in any parkrun so far. This makes it easy to get up a good speed early on and I certainly exploded out of the starting block (speed is relative though, obviously) despite still having a dodgy Achilles tendon. After passing the open grass and finish funnel on the right, the first landmark is the underpass beneath Wells Way which gives you first a slight downhill then uphill (probably the only instance of elevation change throughout the whole course), then you head toward an old train and through the 'Bridge to Nowhere,' (it really does go nowhere) and on along the path until you take a sharp left turn, then another so that you are now on a path parallel to the one you were on moments before but heading in the opposite direction. This straight feels almost as long as the first, but up ahead you will eventually see runners (again, unless you're in first place) turning right and heading toward the lake, which you complete one lap of, before heading back the way you came. This time when you return to the main straight you turn left to the far end of the park, around some cones and then follow the straight all the way back to the finish funnel which you welcome with open arms and pounding lungs.
As I said, I flew (relative, remember) off the start line and was pretty much keeping up with the lead runners until my body realised what was going on and took steps to stop me from doing myself potentially fatal

damage, i.e. I started to slow down. But I didn't slow down as much as I expected to, and in fact my pace all the way around (I didn't check my watch to see exactly what the pace was) felt really strong, despite having reduced my training due to the stupid Achilles tendon being sore.

I finished feeling fresher than usual for a parkrun, and could maybe put this down to Burgess being a very flat course, and/or having more rest than usual during the week. It's hard to say, but one thing's for sure – I really enjoyed the park and the course.

Position: 36 out of 262
Time: 21 minutes 22 seconds.

This meant I was over a minute faster than last week at Orpington, which is incredible, but then the courses are quite different and Burgess seems to be pretty ideal for getting a fast time. The weather was also good, and my foot, despite feeling very sore after the run, felt better during. But still, that's 28 seconds better than the last time I beat my personal best.

Burgess Park is huge, has a lot to see, and is a definite asset to anyone living nearby. I would definitely return and run there again. I have a feeling it will become one of my favourite parkruns after I've been back a couple of times. After the run I headed off to Decathlon, the Achilles tendon feeling very angry (not that I could blame it), first getting lost, then navigating back to the route I'd chosen via Southwark Park. Despite the pain I hobbled into Decathlon and headed over to the running section to look at the gear. How's that for optimism?

## 38. Raphael Park
6th May, 2017
'The not-so-terrible twos'


Preamble

I woke this morning with the alarm, and for some reason thought it was a work day. *6am?* I thought. *Must be a mistake.* Then *Oh . . . Saturday . . . Parkrun . . .* And as usual I was out of bed so quick it was like I'd been jabbed with a cattle prod. It must be because I know how gutted I would be if I nodded off, overslept and ended up missing the parkrun. Something in my brain clicks, whirrs into life and ensures my body and the bed are like two magnets – impossible to join together.
I could very easily have nodded off several times on the train journey. I wished I'd had a biro to hand so I could have jabbed it in my leg to keep me awake – a trick I'd learned at college. But enough nonsense . . .
I had chosen Raphael this week specifically because it was its 2$^{nd}$ birthday. This meant fancy dress was in order, something that always livens up a run. I admit, however, that I didn't have the guts to go dressed up, but fair play to everyone that did.
I had breakfast, dressed and managed to get out of the house more or less on time at 6.45am. The weather was looking ok but still quite cold as I left, and there was hardly a soul about. But then again why would there be at this time on a Saturday? It's not natural. I walked then jogged to the station and caught the waiting Central Line train to Stratford, changing there for an overland train to Gidea Park. I had checked Google Maps beforehand so I knew how to get from Gidea Park station to Raphael Park. I'm not sure how I would do things like this without the internet, specifically Google Maps and TFL. And if I hadn't had time to do it, my phone would have told me all I needed to know. It's easy to take it all for granted.
I recognized the entrance to the park and could already see people arriving, even though it was only 8.30am. There were several people in costume: a Batman or two, a Superman, a Spiderman, a Native American, a couple of nuns and a fairy princess. Raphael parkrun has been going for

two years now and a lot of people had turned up to celebrate. A fantastic spread of cakes, biscuits and home baked treats had been laid out in the bandstand for everyone, and a large crowd had congregated. After some notices and well-deserved awards there was a brief for new runners and then the main brief, then everyone headed up the slope to the start. With no delay we were counted down and off.

The Course

The all-tarmac course starts by heading forward along the perimeter path and turning right, then down a small slope and toward the entrance to the park before taking a hairpin turn to the right to follow the lake before eventually turning right again and heading up a steep but mercifully short slope. At the top the course heads slightly left then right alongside the large playing field for a fairly long stretch before turning left alongside the tennis courts and eventually bearing right to loop clockwise around the playground at the end before heading back along the other side of the tennis courts, with a great view of the runners behind you. At the end of the path a marshal points you to the right to head back the way you came, past the playing field and passing more runners coming toward you. You take a left when you return to the top of the slope and follow the path around the top of the park until you pass the turn-off for the finish funnel and begin the second lap. Once you have completed the second lap and started the third and final one, you keep going as though you are running the same lap as before but this time when you get to the top of the steep slope, instead of turning left toward the playing field and tennis courts, you head right along the top of the park again and turn off near the end of the path toward the finish funnel and (depending on how hard you've pushed yourself) collapse.
I started off fast but knew it wasn't as fast as last week at Burgess Park. It was ok though and I managed to keep up a good pace all the way through the run, despite the legs not feeling too fresh. At least the Achilles tendon wasn't so sore this week. I'm pretty sure I could have pushed myself harder, but I'll save that for another week. No rush. I could maybe have benefitted from more of a warm-up – I had at least half an hour to do it last week and ended up getting an incredible time. Maybe that's the key.

Position: 22 out of 274

Time: 21 minutes 46 seconds.

Not bad. My second best ever time for 5k. I had some of the homemade cake after finishing the run, then headed off toward the tennis courts and the northern park exit. I had intended to run another five miles to Newbury Park station along the A12. Two things stopped me, however. First my Achilles tendon, although not as bad as last week was still store which would have meant a painful few miles when I ultimately didn't have to do them, and secondly I realised I still had my finish token in my pocket . . . D-O-H. I sighed, turned and ran all the way back across the playing field and across the park to queue up and get my barcode and token scanned, then headed off back to Gidea Park station. Surprise, surprise - Raphael is yet another fantastic parkrun course that I'd highly recommend and would love to come back and run again. Happy birthday!

## 39. Lloyd Park
13th May, 2017
'Did I mention I had a bad foot?'

Preamble

So, here's a fact you may not know about Lloyd parkrun: it's difficult (not to mention stupid) to run it when you have Achilles tendonitis. My advice is this: don't run Lloyd parkrun if you have Achilles tendonitis . . . I did it because I'm a fanatic and I'm determined to complete my 47 (Greater London) Parks challenge by mid-July. Lloyd is a great course. It must be if I managed to enjoy it despite being in pain and discomfort. Not only does the course offer a great variety of flat, uphill and downhill in a lovely setting, but there is more than one section where you get to see a line of runners ahead and behind you. Hopefully I'll be back at some point to experience it with two fully functioning feet.

And while we're on the subject - at what point does soreness become an injury? It feels like I'm running with an injury but I know that the foot will feel a lot better tomorrow. It's ironic that only last week I was thinking that my Twitter name 'captainbadfoot' was no longer apt since the chronic sprain had improved so much, but now I have the Achilles tendonitis, the name is appropriate once more.

Anyway, enough moaning. I was out last night, drinking far too much at a company function in the centre of town, getting back home and to bed quite late, having obviously forgotten or stopped caring about the fact that I had to be up at 6am. I didn't quite have a banging hangover, but I did feel a bit weird. And suddenly the idea of traipsing across London (can you traipse in a train?), didn't feel like an entirely pleasant or logical one. I had just enough presence of mind (it was a close thing though) to get myself fed and dressed before leaving the house and heading to the station.

I hadn't done any running at all during the week since a particularly painful run the Sunday before. I was unsure about doing so now but had to find out how the foot was and what my chances would be of getting around Lloyd Park without walking or limping. It was very stiff and sore as I jogged down the road, but I could move on it. So far, so tolerable.

It had been spotting with train, but it eased off as I reached Ealing Broadway where I caught a District Line train to Victoria, arriving just in time to catch a 7.50am train to East Croydon. I got there at around 8.10am and after orientating myself I started walking and running toward the park. The foot had warmed up a bit by now. A bit would have to do. After crossing the tramline I headed into the park and saw a small group of volunteers and runners gathered by the cafe. It looked like they had some refreshments lined up for the end of the run which is always nice to see, and a display copy of Run Director Debra Bourne's *Parkrun: Much More Than Just a Run in the Park*, a great book I read last year and can highly recommend.

I headed up the park to do some warming up, managing a few minutes of running just to see how the foot would react, then headed back to the start where the size of the crowd had increased dramatically. The newcomers were given their brief as I joined the few dozen runners already waiting by the start line. I made sure I positioned myself well back from the front as there was no way in Hell I'd be getting anything close to a PB today. I do like starting further back in the pack sometimes, as you get to enjoy group running, the real essence of parkrun. It was also nice to run at a slower pace than normal . My heart and lungs were certainly relieved and happy, their murmurs of contentment somehow drowning out the sobs and protests of my right foot.

The Course

We were soon off and running, heading first back toward and past the pavilion, then bearing right to head toward a small rise and the bottom right corner of the park. On reaching the corner we turned left, the crowd around me thinning out a bit now, and headed north along the east side of the park before veering left toward a marshal and turning sharp right into an open, rectangular section of the park, heading down to the boundary hedge at the bottom where we turned left along the hedge line, then left again to follow the path by the treeline until it turned right up a fairly steep slope that sent us across grass to a turnaround point, then back to the slope and down via another path to then follow the trees toward the west side of the park, then down the side of the park before taking a left that brought us back to the pavilion and the start of the next lap.

Having warmed up a little bit before the run, the foot wasn't as bad as it could have been, so I had to hold back and just take it easy, contenting myself with just getting around the course without further injury. If I wasn't so keen to finish the 47 Parks challenge, I would have stayed in bed, nursing the foot, as well as the hangover, but that would have meant missing out on Lloyd Park though, and that would have been very sad indeed.

As I not-quite-but-almost hobbled back to East Croydon station, I reminded myself that tomorrow was the first day of my walk along the Thames from the source to the sea. And it would be 23 miles. Maybe it was just the hangover talking, but something told me that due to my ongoing antics (i.e. my refusal to just rest my Achilles tendon and let it heal properly) it might not be an entirely pleasant stroll.

Position: 98 out of 253
Time: 26 minutes 58 seconds.

I wasn't expecting a great time today, and that's fine. And despite the foot, I did enjoy running the parkrun at a slower pace, something I might try to do more often as it's definitely more enjoyable than going all out. I was expecting Lloyd to be an interesting, varied and challenging course, and it was. Not as challenging as Hampstead Heath or Ally Pally maybe, but it certainly requires concentration due to uneven ground in places, and some respect of the hills is advised. It's a really lovely park and a fantastic parkrun. I have a feeling the foot will be ok to walk on tomorrow and for the rest of the Thames hike, I just need to resist the urge to run, which will (as ever) be great. Next week, however, I intend to interrupt the walk to run Gunnersbury parkrun (my local) as it will be my 50th parkrun (in total). I can honestly say I didn't think I'd reach the big 5-0 this quickly, but then I probably didn't expect to become a fanatic . . .

# 40. Gunnersbury Park
20th May, 2017
'No place like home'

Preamble

It felt odd to not be taking part in parkrun as a tourist, but at the same time it was great to finally be back at my home parkrun of Gunnersbury after a year of tourism. In fact my last recorded run there was in September 2015, though I had run the course several times in training since. And the course had altered since then too, due to building works going on in the park. I was amazed to see so many people there, nearly 500 in fact, compared to the 350 the last time I ran. What fantastic weather for it too. There had been a lot of rain in the week, but this morning was absolutely glorious, and the temperature just right.
My feet weren't in great condition. The Sunday before I had started walking the Thames Path national trail. Several very long distances and a whole day of rain at one point had led to soreness and blistering in a couple of places, and a prolonging of the Achilles tendonitis in my right foot. All my fault, no doubt, but there you go. I was wondering if I would even be able to run at Gunnersbury, but a good warm up on the way to the park from West Ealing seemed to do the trick.
I was up at 7.20am, rushing through breakfast and getting dressed so that I could get out of the house for 8.15am. This was probably the latest I had been up for a parkrun, with most of them requiring a 6am start due to the travel. I could get used to this, and no doubt would once the 47 Parks challenge was over. I left the house, the right ankle feeling sore and stiff, and walked down the road then started jogging, stopping when I got to Walpole Park to do some warming up. I carried on, feeling a little better now, and made it to Gunnersbury park for about 8.40am.
Gunnersbury's best feature, as far as I am concerned, is its vast, green open space. I can't think of many other parks in London with such a huge open area. As I waited near the finish funnel, the crowd grew and there seemed to be a constant stream of approaching runners, stretching into the distance.

There was a pre-run briefing with some announcements, then we all turned and walked a short way down the path to the start line. I still couldn't get over how many people were there, more than most of the parkruns I'd been to. In fact the numbers probably only compared to Richmond and Bushy, but I could be wrong. I couldn't hear the countdown, but knew it had happened when everyone around me lurched forward.

The Course

From the start line the course heads west along the north perimeter path to the main entrance, where it turns left and continues following the outer path as it now heads south and slightly downhill. After a while the path heads into trees with the open green still on the left, and eventually comes to a left turn by the Potomac fish pond, going straight before taking another left turn, now heading uphill, back up the park on the other side of the green, past the pavillion until it comes to a right turn where it heads around the golf course to the Round Pond. The course now curves gradually around to the right, passing the café and the museum, then curves left, then right again, now following the path along the bottom of the park for a good distance before turning right and heading up the west side of the park and ultimately past the main entrance again, turning right to head along the top of the park to the finish funnel and a lot of panting, but relieved runners.

Despite the sore feet and Achilles problem I ran faster than I expected, and although I didn't break any personal records, I was very happy with the result. Also, after spending most of the week hiking solo it was good to be back in a crowd again. A great atmosphere and a great course.

Position: 79 out of 499
Time: 22 minutes 33 seconds.

Gunnersbury is one of those fairly rare one-lap parkrun courses. It does double back on itself at the end, but given the beauty of the park, this doesn't feel like a hardship. I've now run Gunnersbury more than any other parkrun (it was currently tied with Bushy at three runs each), and once my 47 Parks challenge is over I'll be looking forward to coming back again and again. The scenery on offer in the park is superb, the central green space stunning in its vastness, and the crowd and enthusiasm is immense. It's never been more inspiring to come home.

## 41. Bromley
27th May, 2017
'A very peculiar marathon'

Preamble

I have to say I was dreading parkrun this week. Not because of where it was, or the nature of the course, or the weather or anything like that, but because physically I was in 'a right state.' I still had the Achilles tendonitis that had been plaguing me for several weeks, but I was also several days into my Thames Path walk, where each day averaged twenty miles. My legs and feet were taking a pounding. Today would be the last stretch of the trail, from Putney to the Thames Barrier, but I would have to do the parkrun first. I had initially thought the walk to be 15 miles, but it ended up being over 23. So altogether today involved a marathon, albeit a very odd one . . . With only three miles actual running. Although last week's parkrun at Gunnersbury had been ok, I was concerned that all the relentless walking and my refusal to let my tendonitis heal (apart from a couple of rest days in the middle of the walk), would put me closer to injury than ever before, and although I was determined to rein myself in and run slowly this week, I still thought there was a chance that I might not be able to run at all. I would have to see.
I woke at 6am and had breakfast, making sure all the gear I needed was packed in my rucksack for the parkrun and the walk afterwards. Thankfully with the final stretch being in London there was no need to pack too much food as it was readly available. The weather looked ok, just a bit more overcast than the day before which had been glorious. I left the house in good time but resisted jogging to the station. I needed to do the absolute minimum of running to ensure my feet got me through the parkrun.
I caught a District Line train to Victoria from Ealing Broadway and then caught an earlier than planned train from Victoria to Bromley South which turned out to be the first stop. Leaving the station at Bromley I checked my position on my phone and navigated my way to Norman Park, a fairly long walk but straightforward. There were some grey clouds overhead,

and it did start to spot with rain, but thankfully it didn't progress to a full-on shower.

When I reached the park I could see the car park was filling up and several groups of people were arriving or warming up, even with half an hour still to go to the start of the run. I walked along to the finish funnel and dropped my bag off before jogging down the path a little way. The heel was stiff, sore and reluctant, as I knew it would be, but with a little more light running and some stretching it felt like it would be ok.

I could see a lot of runners arriving and crossing the park now, so I headed back toward the entrance, then left along the path to where people were gathering near the start. There was indeed a large crowd, and what looked like a fairly constant stream of arrivals, right up until the countdown. I headed over to the run briefing for newcomers and tourists and learned that the current course is the dry, summer alternative, which hasn't been used for a while. A few minutes later the countdown was shouted out and everyone got going, a massive group of people that to anyone who hadn't witnessed parkrun before or even heard of it (if there even are such people) must have looked pretty impressive.

The Course

The course starts in the southwest corner of the park near the athletics track and heads north up the grass to the top of the park where it joins the path and turns right, heading past the pavilion before turning right off the path and following the dog-leg of trees almost to the bottom of the park before turning left and heading up the other side and turning right as it hits the path again. It then, briefly follows the path again before turning right and following the trees on the northeast side of the park, curving around the car park and bearing right to follow the bottom path, passing both pavilions until it reaches the athletics track again where it starts lap two. The third lap is only half a lap and takes you from the start line, around the top path to the second pavilion and the finish funnel.

I ran tentatively from the start, averaging a 7 and a half minute pace which remained consistent for pretty much most of the run. It was painful with the heel, but I was determined not to slow down too much or stop. I certainly wasn't as fast as I was at Gunnersbury Park the week before, but all the hiking was probably the cause of that. My poor, poor heel. What it has had to put up with.

Position: 144 out of 555
Time: 23 minutes 37 seconds.

Well, it was a long way from being one of my best times, but since the idea was just to turn up and run the course today without doing myself an injury or tiring myself out before the rest of the day's activity, I can't be disappointed. The Norman Park course is obviously popular, given the number of people who turned up, and it's not difficult to see why. If I had been in better condition I'd have enjoyed it a lot more. It's flat, has great surfaces to run on, and like a good book it has just enough twists and turns to keep you interested. Yet again it was nice to run at a slightly slower pace and feel more like part of the crowd. That is, after all, what it's all about.

It took me a while to get to Putney to continue and finish my Thames Path walk. It was hard work and I didn't finish it until after 6pm, but it was good to be done, and also good to know that I had completed the whole walk without missing a parkrun.

## 42. Greenwich
3rd June, 2017
'What I dream about when I dream about parkrun'


Preamble

Although I had finished the last day of my Thames Path walk last Saturday and had done nothing remotely energetic since, I still felt exhausted today. It may be the culmination of the 200 miles of walking still having an effect, or it may have been the hot nights making it difficult to sleep, but either way it was difficult to keep my eyes open on the train journey to Greenwich. Luckily for me, running is one of those activities I can motivate myself to do regardless of how tired I feel. A lot of it is just forward momentum, not that much effort needed. It's when you have to run fast and for long distances where it can get tricky. So although I could have done with going back to bed I knew I should be okay for this morning's parkrun, provided my Achilles tendonitis didn't stop me. I had tried a couple of test runs around an empty floor at work during the week and the pain did flare up, but it receded fairly quickly too.
The alarm went off at 6am waking me, ironically, from a dream about parkrun. The dream had taken place in a park I'd never been to before on a grey, drizzly morning. The lead runners had come around to lap me after what seemed like only seconds from the start of the run, and I soon found myself alone, heading out into woodland and realising I must have missed a turn somewhere, and wondering where all the marshals and, come to think of it, the rest of the runners were. No dream PB for me then.
Back in the real world I roused myself and got dressed, trying to work out if I'd forgotten to pack anything. Although I'd completed the Thames Path - walking the length of the river from the source to the Thames Barrier, I'd intended to walk the rest of the way to where it meets the sea, and today I'd planned to walk from the Barrier, via the Thames Path extension to Erith. Was I really going to be bothered? I decided to wait until after the parkrun to see how I felt.
I left the house and walked to the station, catching a Central Line train to Bond Street, then changing to the Jubilee Line to get to London Bridge

where I caught an overland train to Falconwood. I'm always surprised by how tight they are with leg space on these trains. It is literally impossible to sit in the seat properly without causing myself significant pain. How people taller than me are supposed to cope I don't know. It almost makes standing preferable. I left the train and the station, tempted to get a coffee but realising I didn't have as much time as I had expected, and walked down the road to the entrance to Avery Hill Park. The weather was, as promised, sunny with a fair amount of cloud. I walked across the park to the café to find a small group already gathered, dropped my bag and had a bit of a stretch and a warm-up. There wasn't a lot of time left, and I didn't anticipate a fast time anyway, so the exercises were more out of routine than anything. It was then time for the run briefing which led swiftly into the countdown and the start of the run.

The Course

From the Avery Hill Park café the course heads roughly southwest, passing the tennis court on the left, then taking a sharp left to follow the line of trees almost to the bottom of the park but taking a left, then right turn before hitting the path where a marshal is stationed. The course then follows the footpath along the bottom of the park before eventually turning left near the Avery Hill Road entrance and further on heading slightly uphill then northeast until it almost reaches the top path, but instead heading across the grass all the way back to the start to begin lap two. For the third lap, runners head through the finish funnel part way across the grass instead of back toward the café.

I was just happy that my foot didn't call a halt to proceedings this week, though I won't lie – I wish the damned thing would hurry up and heal. I, like a lot of runners, am very impatient with injuries. I want to let it heal, but I don't want to stop running and lose fitness. A frustrating and potentially damaging paradox. Hey ho.

Position: 46 out of 203
Time: 23 minutes 40 seconds.

So the time was more or less the same as last week at Bromley. I could have run faster if my foot wasn't so sore, so it was a balance of trying not to run too slowly and trying not to run too fast and risk making the foot worse. Greenwich (Avery Hill Park) is a great course. It's a fairly straightforward lap with a little uphill and downhill mixed in, and a fair amount of running on soft, flat grass in pleasant surroundings. Highly recommended. I'm beginning to think I'll never find a parkrun I can actually criticise, but hey, that's nothing to complain about.

And in case you're wondering – I didn't go to the Thames Barrier to continue the walk. The brain was willing but the body was having none of it. Actually, I'm not even sure the brain was willing . . .

## 43. Peckham Rye
10th June, 2017
'The Hangover – Parts 1, 2 and 3'


Preamble

Ok, so I could have felt worse but boy was it hard work this week. I normally try to avoid drinking alcohol the night before a parkrun but I thought I would have a few this week to celebrate a colleague's birthday and, inevitably, a few turned into quite a few, which turned into a few too many. Although I didn't get home disastrously late, I didn't get anywhere near as much sleep as my lager-poisoned body demanded, so that I woke at 6am to find myself laughing at the alarm clock. It had to be a joke. It wasn't. I dragged myself out of bed and took manual control of my body since attempting to do anything on autopilot would have led to bizarre and potentially fatal results. I downed a smoothie and coffee (solids a bit too much for my stomach at this point) and sat on the edge of the bed knowing that if I were to lie back for just one second I would be consumed by an immediate and deep sleep. And while this concerned me, it was also very tempting. But given how cross I would be with myself later at missing a parkrun I would just have to endure the exhaustion and nausea and get on with things. Besides, today was Peckham Rye, one of five parkruns left to do in my 47 Parks challenge. I was so close to the finish now. Too close to mess things up.
I somehow got myself organised and out of the house on time and headed down the road to Ealing Broadway where I caught a Central Line train to Bond Street, a Jubilee Line train to Canada Water (no time to visit Decathlon this week, sadly) then an overground train to Honour Oak Park. When I got to Honour Oak Park I was in dire need of the toilet, a situation no doubt brought on by the 'celebrations' yesterday and which worsened quickly. I decided to turn in to the nearby park and see if there was a loo there, but it soon became apparent that I was out of luck and fast approaching a situation I could describe as 'total crisis.' I then spotted another church-like building at the end of the park (which turned out to be the crematorium). It was simple – if this building didn't have an

accessible toilet I would have to improvise, a word I won't (for the benefit of anyone reading this) elaborate on. Luckily it did have a toilet, which was actually palatial compared to most public conveniences, and so disaster was averted.

Outside I checked my phone to see where I was in relation to the park, and although I could have gotten there fairly quickly from where I was, I ended up retracing my steps and getting to the park the long way round. Still, I had enough time so it wasn't a problem.

At the bottom of the road I found the entrance to the park and was encouraged to see several other runners about. I quickly found the gathering point near the finish funnel and dropped my bag by the fence. Oddly I forgot to stretch this week, but considering the poor state my mind and body were in, I'm not surprised, and don't think it would have made much difference anyway – if any week was absolutely not going to be a PB week, it was this one. My Achilles tendonitis seemed a bit better, but it was still stopping me from running as fast as I would like, and because my running had dropped off due to the near-injury, I wasn't in top shape. Still, the important thing was to just get around, and the slower pace was enjoyable. I joined in the briefing for visitors and first time parkrunners, learning about the various features along the course, of which there are quite a few. Then it was time for the general briefing and we were off. The sky had now brightened considerably and the temperature had risen. All morning I had been thirsty, due to the hangover, but what was strange was that after the run the thirst had gone rather than gotten worse.


The Course

The Peckham Rye course begins on wide path in the middle of the open grass area, and soon takes a left turn and heads roughly northwest, continuing ahead at a crossroads and soon bearing left to head toward and around the oval-shaped ornamental garden. It then follows the River Peck and passes the bowling green. There are then two left turns in quick succession before turning around the pond and then following a loop around the Small Acres School, before heading back out onto the open grass on a path toward Colyton Road, turning right and heading back toward the start point to begin lap two.

I started off nice and easy then increased my pace a little, conscious not to get too carried away, bearing in mind I was hungover and delicate as well as nursing a sore ankle. I really enjoyed the many twists and turns of the course, and given the many features of the park, I can see how any route around it would be varied and interesting. It is almost completely flat, and the surface is good. Although there were other people out enjoying the park and the weather it certainly didn't feel congested and everyone seemed to be having a great time. I'd be more than happy if this was my local.

Position: 56 out of 183
Time: 23 minutes 42 seconds.

I was content to be under twenty-four minutes, and to be honest, trying to get anything faster than that in my condition would have been foolhardy. I really do want to get back to faster times, but trying to overrule or ignore your body is never a good idea. I'll just have to keep being patient. There are only four more Greater London parkruns to go in my challenge now, just one month (all being well) until I can say I'm 'Lon-done.'

## 44. Grovelands
17th June, 2017
'Not long now . . .'


Preamble

Thankfully I didn't have to battle an awful hangover this week. But although I got to sleep ok the night before, I could have done with more rest. I don't think I'll ever get used to getting up earlier on a Saturday than I do during the week, but with the 'Lon-Done' challenge drawing to a close, I knew I wouldn't have to do it for much longer. The alarm was more of a shock than expected though. Normally the artificial daylight it creates wakes me up gradually, but this time waking up was like being slapped in the face. It's a good job that I have a repetitive piano tune as an alarm, rather than a radio. If it was something I'd actually like to listen to I'd probably fall straight back to sleep. I stopped the alarm, grunted something incoherent, got out of bed before my eyelids could close again then went to sort out some breakfast. My foot had felt better during the week but it was still sore and I was now sure that it would stay that way until I could take a couple of weeks off running altogether.
Leaving the flat on time at about 6.50am, I walked to Ealing Broadway where I caught a Central Line train to Oxford Circus, then a Victoria Line train to Highbury and Islington, where I caught a National Rail train to Winchmore Hill. The trains, in general, seemed busier than usual for this time on a Saturday morning. Some people were obviously going to work but there appeared to be more tourists about, perhaps because of the great weather which today was particularly hot and sunny.
I left the station, checked my phone to see which way I had to go to get to Grovelands Park, went the wrong way, corrected myself and walked up Broad Walk, turning right into Branscombe Gardens, at the end of which was a wooded path that led into the park. I stopped to take some photos and videos, then headed along the path to the gathering point near the boating lake. I found the loo and had a very short warm-up run but it wasn't really enough. Time seems to go so quickly on these parkrun mornings. I dropped my bag by a hedge near the gathering point and at

some point a marshal must have moved it from there to the finishing point. It's a good job they were more concerned about it than I was. Thank you to whoever it was.

Soon everyone was gearing up to go and I listened in on the newcomers' briefing to get an idea of the course which is relatively straightforward. I then joined the main group with a minute or two to go, soon realising I was at the front of the crowd facing everyone else, so got out of the way and joined somewhere in the middle. A few minutes later, after the main briefing, we all set off, a bigger group than I had expected. I was feeling very comfortable with the starting pace, so I sped up and moved on to the grass on the left side of the path to move up to something more like my average pace.

The Course

The roughly speech bubble-shaped course begins at the north side of the boating lake in a small group of trees, and heads northeast along the perimeter path in a long anti-clockwise curve, passing the tennis courts and heading uphill to the top of the park where the course turns back the way it came, following a long straight section until it's time to turn left and slowly descend back toward the boating lake, but continuing on along the path, bearing right and going around a small roundabout just beyond where some marshals are gathered to cheer runners on. At the end of this stretch there is a sharp, hairpin turn to the left which takes you back to the path alongside the boating lake, past the entrance to the finish funnel and eventually onto lap two. The next lap is identical, but on the third lap you turn into the finish funnel about a third of the way along the lake.

Although I started off quite slow, I did pick up speed and, even with the uphill section, still managed to do better than last week. But considering how hungover I was last week, this might not be saying much. I did feel I could have run faster though, so maybe next week will bring something like a return to form, provided my foot can handle it.

Position: 34 out of 162
Time: 23 minutes, 29 seconds

One of the great things about the Grovelands course, like a number of others, is that on some stretches you can see people ahead of and behind you. And at the end of the run, if you have time to stick around, you're given the perfect vantage point for watching runners approach the finish funnel or embark on their last lap. It's a great course - straightforward with just the right amount of up and downhill in lovely surroundings. I now have only three more parkruns to go before I've completed every single one in Greater London.

## 45. Gladstone
24th June, 2017
'Aloha!'


Preamble

Now that the temperature had dropped, sleeping was easier. Sleeping had been hard work for the whole country due to the hot weather this week. I had been more tired last night (Friday) than I can remember, finding myself dropping off in front of the TV which I very rarely do. But despite a cooler, more restful night I still had to face the usual early Saturday start, and I woke at 6.30am asking myself serious existential questions.
I got up, ate, dressed and went over the travel plan in my head which was actually pretty straightforward. I had intended to run Gladstone Park (named after the British prime minister William Gladstone) last week but when I realised that it was their five year anniversary this week with an Hawaiian theme, I decided to delay it. I still had the Achilles tendonitis but I had managed to get in two runs during the week rather than the usual one, and when the pain grew too much to bear this time I tried running without the ankle strap which I had originally started wearing for the chronic sprain in the same foot. The difference and relief was immediate and I wondered if in fact the strap itself had been the cause of the tendonitis in the first place. Typical – the solution of one problem is the cause of the next. Saying that, the tendon was really stiff this morning making me think I'd been a bit overzealous on the last training run, strap or not. But sure enough, after warming up later it would prove to feel better than it had in weeks.
I left the flat at 7.20am and walked down to West Ealing station to catch a 7.26am train to Paddington, where I caught a Bakerloo Line train to Baker Street and changed to the Jubilee Line to get to Willesden Green. I arrived at about 8.10am with plenty of time, and jogged to the park in less than ten minutes. When I got to Gladstone Park I could see a couple of volunteers already setting up the finish funnel, so I headed over to the finish area where a table was being set up with melon, bananas and other goodies, and dropped my bag by the café. I then headed off, following the

course markers to get an idea of the course and see a bit more of the park. I wasn't expecting the uphill section, so I was glad I was scoping it out in advance and saving myself the potentially unpleasant surprise later on. But it isn't that steep, and like any uphill, how hard it is depends on how fast you're going. I reached the top of the hill near the Stable café and the remains of Dollis Hill House, then turned and followed another path, heading eventually back to the other café as it was getting close to 9am. A lot of runners had gathered now, some wearing Hawaiian gear and getting into the spirit of things. The sky had been grey all morning, but although a few errant drops of rain were felt, it stayed dry and even seemed to be clearing up a couple of times.

There was a briefing for first-timers followed by an entertaining briefing for everyone, recognising the park's impressive five year history, and everyone who had helped bring it to life and keep it going. We then walked to the start point not far from the Park Avenue North entrance, and with little more ado were counted down.

The Course

The course begins on the path not far from the entrance and heads straight up to the top of the park where it turns left, going up and across the bridge over the railway track, then continuing uphill on the tree-lined path before taking a left turn, followed shortly by another one, curving down to a crossroads where it turns right and follows a long curving path, going uphill again before it reaches another corner by Dollis Hill Lane where it turns left and then left again, going downhill now by a vast, open stretch of grass. Near Mulgrave Road the course turns left and follows the south path before heading northeast to meet the crossroads again by the playground, but turning right (avoiding other runners) and heading back down to the bridge where it turns left and begins the second lap. Once you have completed the second lap, you head back over the bridge and retrace your steps to the start point, turning left by the marshal and striking out across the grass toward the welcoming finish funnel.

Having had a good warm up, my sore ankle was in good shape for the whole run, and although I took it relatively easy all the way around, never pushing myself, I still felt I'd put in a better performance than the past few weeks. There was more uphill than the previous few parkruns, but I never felt like it was slowing me down. In the briefing for newcomers the director had said that although there are hills on the course, the course will look after you. Having run the course, I think I know what he means.

Time: 23 minutes, 17 seconds
Position: 48 out of 207

It's nowhere near my best time, but it's the fastest I've run since Gunnersbury Park a month ago. Hopefully it's a sign that the tendon is healing. I can happily recommend Gladstone Park to any would-be tourists. There is a great mix of flat, uphill and downhill running, plenty of twists and turns and scenery to look at, and a huge open section in the latter part of the lap to make you feel like you're no longer in the city but out in the countryside. There is a friendly crowd and let's face it – if it's been going for five years it must be doing something right.

## 46. Wimbledon
1st July, 2017
'Underground, over ground'


Preamble

The approaching end to my 47 Parks challenge was on my mind all week. Barring the extension to the challenge i.e. park number 48, South Norwood, I was only two parks from completion, and the whole scope of the challenge, how long it had taken, what I had done and where I had been in over a year, was starting to dawn on me. I was also starting to feel a little sad that it was all coming to an end, but all good things must.
I had been looking forward to Wimbledon Common parkrun for some time. I've been to the common a number of times in the past, and had checked out the course a month ago while training for a long hike along the Thames. The only worry I'd had was the potential for mud, but although it had been raining this week, the ground wasn't too bad at all, and off-road shoes weren't necessary. If you are heading to Wimbledon for the first time, however, it is worth considering the weather and taking off-road shoes with you if practical. That said, it's only a couple of stretches that are really susceptible to heavy rainfall, so nothing to be concerned about.
I woke at 6.15am and got up to see light grey cloud through the window. So long as it wasn't raining this was fine with me. Again, it's amazing how few times it has rained on Saturday mornings while running parkrun. Crystal Palace was the only occasion when rain was really noticeable, but even then it wasn't able to spoil the experience. I ate and dressed and was out of the house in good time, heading down the road for a warm-up run to Ealing Broadway station. After making the decision to run without an ankle support in the last week, my Achilles tendonitis had improved a little, and I was able to start running faster again. On the run to the station I could feel that my foot was coping better and complaining less. Provided I had an ample warm up for the run today I reckoned I could be on for another fast time, even if I had no chance of getting near my parkrun PB.

I took a District Line train to Earl's Court and changed there for another District Line train to Wimbledon Park station, getting there at about 8am. It was only a short walk from there to Wimbledon Park itself, but when I got there I found the gate padlocked. The plan had been to follow the Capital Ring signs from there to the common, but without access to the park, this wasn't possible, so I continued up the road intending to divert around the park and maybe pick up the Capital Ring somewhere further on. After another good warm up run I stopped and checked the map on my phone – a good idea since I could easily have gone wrong if I hadn't. I turned down a side road and past some shops, and was soon running alongside the common itself, heading all the way to the end of the road before turning left into the trees where I tripped on a tree root and went flying.

After dusting myself down and looking around to see if anyone had noticed (no one had, thank God) I headed on along the path toward the windmill, to find that several groups of runners had already arrived.

I dropped my bag by a tree and a group of welcoming volunteers, and headed off onto the course itself for some more warming up. I had it in my head that it was a clockwise run, perhaps because that's the way I went around when I checked it out a few weeks ago, but it's actually anti-clockwise. I did some stretching, seeing more people warming up, then headed back to the start where a few hundred keen runners were now assembled. After some notices and milestone announcements from the run director it was time to get cracking.

The Course

From the gathering area near the windmill and car park, runners walk along the wooded path to the start line chalked on the ground. From here the course heads back down toward the gathering area and finish funnel, turning left at the end and heading back up the common on another long wooded path parallel to the A219 before eventually turning left, then left again and soon running alongside the King's Mere Lake before turning left and heading down the long, tree-lined path, avoiding the odd tree root and mud patch and eventually crossing over the start line again and beginning the second lap. At the end of the second lap, the course continues on to the gathering area again, entering the finish funnel instead of turning left. There are helpful white, chalk arrows on the ground at key points, as well as volunteers to ensure you don't get lost in the trees, end up in the lake etc. Not that that's likely.

Due to Wimbledon's popularity there were a lot of runners lined up at the start, so it took a while to get through the crowd and run at a challenging pace. Once there though I was surprised at how well I maintained a relatively fast pace, possibly due to the speed-training I'd started up again during the week. I could definitely have pushed myself harder, and if I was running the course again, I would have the advantage of knowing what to expect.

Time: 22 minutes, 42 seconds
Position: 85 out of 405

The improvement in performance and time continues, despite the Achilles tendonitis still being with me. I'm really looking forward to the finale of my challenge at Bushy Park next week, and reckon I can get an even faster time, something close to my parkrun PB. Wimbledon is one of the oldest parkrun courses, and I can see why it's one of the most popular. The ground is soft, the paths are wide and the terrain/scenery is varied and interesting. There are no uphill sections, so provided the ground isn't too wet there is a great opportunity for getting a PB if that's what you're after. If it's your first foray into parkrun, the course and whole Wimbledon experience will guarantee that it won't be your last. And as for Wombles? Well, I did see a couple of small creatures scurry off into the undergrowth at one point, but they were surely too small to be wombles. Saying that, I didn't spot any litter on the common. . .

## 47. Bushy Park
8th July, 2017
'The beginning'


Preamble

It felt good, and at the same time quite strange, to think that it was all coming to an end. In one way it wasn't really ending at all – South Norwood, the 48th Greater London parkrun was starting the same day I was running Bushy, and Hoblingwell was due to start the week after, but I had always planned for the last parkrun of my personal challenge to be Bushy. It made sense for me to stop where parkrun had begun, and with what must be the biggest average attendance of any London parkrun. Besides, with the rate that new parkruns were springing up, the challenge could have dragged on forever. I will definitely get to the new ones, but with a little less urgency than before. It was time for a rest.
My brother Darryl had driven down from Ludlow to support me on the final parkrun of the challenge. It was quite fitting since he was the one who had introduced me to parkrun a few years back and had encouraged me to go with him to Bushy Park. It felt like it had all come full circle. Here we were again at Bushy Park. Only now I was doing it with the experience of fifty or so other parkruns behind me.
The course had changed since the first time I had been there, and due to me misjudging how far I had run (I don't like looking at my watch during the run as it nearly always has bad news for me) I left the final sprint to the finish too late, but at least this meant I had more in the tank if I had needed it, which was good. And considering I had the Ludlow 10k later in the day this wasn't a bad thing. It also meant that I was probably fitter than I thought after the slump in training due to the Achilles tendonitis. I was never going to get a PB this week, but that didn't matter, what mattered was enjoying the last run of what had been a very long series.
The recent heatwave had made sleeping difficult over the past few nights, but I felt ok when the alarm went off, probably because the sun had slowly woken me up over the previous hour. I got up got dressed, had breakfast then checked I had everything I needed in my rucksack. Darryl

had been kipping in the living room and was also now up. He was going to cycle back to where he had left his car in Hampton while I would catch a 65 bus from Ealing Broadway to Kingston and walk to Bushy Park from there where we would meet up.

For practically the whole journey I was thinking about timing and how I would feel if for some reason I got to Bushy Park late or not at all. This was the day I had chosen to end the challenge. If it didn't go to plan I'd have to wait at least a week to try again, at which point South Norwood would be the 48th Greater London parkrun, and the compulsion to add it to my challenge would be hard to ignore. Luckily the journey was quicker than I expected and with no hold-ups I got off the bus at Kingston station at about 8.15am, to head in the direction of the bridge.

Finding Bushy Park was fairly straightforward and I was soon following the path along the edge of the King's Field, seeing a herd of deer grazing nearby as I headed in the direction of the car park. I got there and found Darryl. Even though there was still twenty minutes to go the area was very busy and a crowd of runners had already formed at the top of the avenue near the Diana fountain. I warmed up a little, did some stretching, then headed over to the start. The number of people there was immense compared to every other parkrun I've been to, but this was no surprise. Looking at the results pages for Bushy you will see that the number of runners is regularly over a thousand, with it rarely dipping below 900. This is where it all began with Paul Sinton-Hewitt and friends in 2004. This still felt very much like the beating heart of parkrun, a Mecca where every tourist would have to come sooner or later. The run director went through his messages then we were moving, slowly at first, then into a light jog, then a run. There were voices, there was puffing and panting, and under it all a steady, thundering rhythm. The rhythm of a stampede. A stampede of good will, of shared interest and the pursuit of positive change, improved fitness. It was a glorious sound.

Further on I drew alongside a group of men dressed in old military uniforms. I can't remember what they were supporting or commemorating, but fair play to them – they must have been sweltering. They looked happy though.


The Course

Once you reach the end of the avenue, the course hits Cobbler's Walk then heads roughly East until it reaches Hampton Wick Royal Cricket Club where it turns left, then soon afterwards turns right before turning left again then heading northwest in the direction of Leg of Mutton Pond. Just beyond the pond it turns sharp right and heads all the way to Sandy Lane, where it turns left and runs parallel to Sandy Lane all the way to Chestnut Avenue where it turns left and follows the avenue for over a third of its length before turning left again back onto Cobbler's Walk. It now heads back in the direction of Leg of Mutton Pond, but turns right before it gets there and follows a curving path toward Heron Pond, passing over the small bridge, and following the outside of the pond all the way to the finish funnel.

As well as being a beautiful location anyway, Bushy Park also has a fantastic one-lap course. I haven't run this configuration before, otherwise I'd have known when to speed up near the end and sprint into the finish funnel. Although it did take a couple of minutes to really get going at the start due to the large crowd, I wasn't really held back, and it didn't affect my overall time. I still achieved a time I am happy with.

If you live locally to Bushy Park, and it was the only park you had ever run, you would have a good reason to be content. It's a beautiful place with a great course and is extremely popular, so wherever you are on the course, and whatever speed you are moving at, you're unlikely to be alone. That said, there are so many other parkruns out there, London itself having 47, sorry – 48 . . . Actually it might be 50+ by the time you read this, but . . . Numbers aren't important, are they? Just bear in mind that with parkrun the numbers are likely to grow and keep growing. It doesn't look like they're going to drop any time soon. Speaking of numbers . . .

Time: 22 minutes 28 seconds
Position: 165 out of 927

There is definitely the sense of an ending. I will be running South Norwood (number 48) and Hoblingwell (number 49) soon. But as far as the challenge goes I had to draw the line somewhere, and Bushy was the best place to do so. I'm Lon-done for now. It's been a very, very long challenge. I began last June, over a year ago and, with very few exceptions, have run a different parkrun every week, getting up earlier than was sensible to trek across the capital. It has been an exercise in self-discipline, but it has paid off. I have seen more of London than I ever thought I would, and I have been amazed at how many fantastic parks and green spaces are in this city alone. We are utterly spoiled, and we should all be getting out and enjoying these places more. Who knows, they may not be around forever. After South Norwood and Hoblingwell I have a few more parkruns I'd like to visit, but I think I'll hold off on setting myself any more challenges for a while. It's nice to be flexible.

## 48. Hoblingwell
25th November, 2017
'Cold open'


Preamble

So more than four months had passed since completing my 47 Parks challenge in Bushy Park in July, and all through that time South Norwood and Hoblingwell had been on my mind. Neither had been part of that challenge that I had set myself, but I still felt obligated to run them nonetheless. Perhaps this was because, after all, as a parkrunner I could only truly say I was 'Lon-Done' if I had genuinely run all the current, active London parkruns. It was something that required updating. So I decided to do Hoblingwell first, for no other reason that it had an interesting name, and despite a couple of failures to get up the previous weeks (once due to not setting my alarm, another time because I just couldn't motivate myself) I managed to organise myself and get up at 6am to have time to get ready and make the journey across London.
I knew it would be cold, but I didn't anticipate how cold. I was wearing three top layers – a t-shirt (my 50 parkrun milestone t-shirt that had come a few weeks ago and which I had been waiting eagerly for), a long sleeve top, and a long-sleeve, hooded top. I thought this would be enough, but it wasn't as it turned out, and I should definitely have added a fleece top in there, particularly for the journey back when I was cold and damp from perspiration. I did think about wearing track pants too, and decided not to – another mistake – as this too would have helped keep me a bit warmer. Thankfully I did take a hat and gloves at least, as even with the gloves my fingertips froze and it was only after the run that they warmed up again.
Leaving the flat at about 6.45am, I headed past people setting up the vintage market along the avenue, and headed down the road toward Ealing Broadway, breaking into a light warm-up run. By the time I reached the station I was pretty much on time, and saw a waiting District Line train, so sped up to get on it before it left. I was hoping it was an earlier one than the one I was meant to catch, and it probably was, but due to a delay from signal failure it didn't end up leaving the station until about

twenty minutes later, leaving me concerned that I would get to Victoria station too late for my connecting train. I checked for the next train after that from Victoria. It would be another half an hour, which would leave me with only minutes to get to Hoblingwell parkrun from St Mary Cray station. Luckily, when I got to Victoria and checked the board, the 7.52 train was delayed to 7.56, the precious four minutes probably meaning the difference between me catching and missing the train. I boarded, and the train was soon making its way out of Victoria and across the river into South London toward Brixton.

Everywhere there was grass there was frost, though this wouldn't be made fully apparent until I reached Hoblingwell Wood Recreation Ground. When the train reached St Mary Cray station I disembarked, gratefully found the toilets, then left the station, walking across a particularly icy bridge, but appreciating the view of the sunrise and low clouds in the distance. I passed a café where some workmen were eating breakfast. They looked about as warm and comfortable as I wasn't. I crossed the road and continued up the hill to the recreation ground where two police officers were hanging around by their car. The ground itself is a large open stretch of grass, surrounded by houses, but being so high up it gives a great impression of space, and doesn't feel hemmed in. There is a clubhouse and a small wood behind it, giving a nice variety of terrain in a relatively small area. I walked around to the starting point of the run and dropped my bag in the frost-covered grass, before setting off for a warm up. The ground was quite muddy in places, particularly heading into the wood, but it wasn't too bad, and the sun was growing stronger, slowly warming things up a bit, so that when I made my way back to the start I took off my outer, upper layer.

More people had gathered now, all looking keen and positive, despite the cool weekend morning. There were around fifty in total, most of whom seemed to be newcomers. After a short briefing we walked to the start point and were off.

The Course

The lap begins near the clubhouse and heads roughly south, completing an anti-clockwise circuit of the south field, then starting on a second circuit, but heading onto the path instead of returning to the start again, turning right, in front of the clubhouse and heading north before turning left, crossing a path and heading up a short slope, before turning back on itself and turning right to run parallel to the road (Leesons Way) and heading up the hill before turning right, and down into the wooded section. This was the muddy section, though since it didn't last too long it didn't present too much of a problem. Once out of the wood the route turns left along the base of the small hill, then right to follow the long stretch along the perimeter of the north field, all the way to Chipperfield Road where it turns right, then right again toward the clubhouse. Here the course turns right, and repeats the section up the small hill, toward and along the road and through the wood. After heading along the north field perimeter a second time, and turning right, back toward the clubhouse, you turn left and complete a final lap of the south field, heading into the finish funnel at the end, not far from the start.

At the beginning of the run I had more or less been one of the front runners, but my speed had soon slowed, and my lack of speed training in the previous few weeks began to take its toll as I dropped to a slower, more comfortable pace. The terrain and the cold may well have played their part in the disappointing time, but my fitness definitely felt like the root cause.

Time: 24 minutes 48 seconds
Position: 21 out of 53

So I wasn't far off 25 minutes. This was easily one of my worst parkrun times. It makes sense though – I had missed a few parkruns in the previous few weeks, and my speed wasn't what it had been during my original 47 Parks challenge, certainly nowhere near my best time of 21 minutes 22 seconds at Burgess parkrun at the end of April. But this was good – it was a wake-up call. It showed me that I had work to do to get back to my peak, and I was now motivated to do so. 21 minutes 22 seconds would be tough to beat in perfect weather on a flat course, but I was determined to do it on any course, even in the dead of winter. It was unlikely that I would do it at South Norwood, as that was only a week away, but I would do it. Speaking of which, after completing South Norwood I would be Lon-Done again. I could finally get rid of that niggle that had plagued me since Bushy Park. There were now rumblings of a 50th London parkrun. Maybe there would be no end. Maybe being 'Lon-Done' can only ever be temporary. We shall see.

## 49. South Norwood
3rd December, 2017
'Lon-done again'

Preamble

Getting up for parkrun last week had been difficult after a long break from tourism, and so it was this week, though at least it wasn't as much of a shock to the system. It wasn't quite as cold as last week either. So here I was, getting up and getting dressed for the last of the Greater London parkruns. Bushy Park had meant the end of my '47 Parks' challenge, but the sting in the tail – finding out that South Norwood was starting on the day I finished my challenge, had soured the victory a little. Part of me felt like I'd done what I'd set out to do and that was that, while another part of me had felt that, technically, I hadn't finished – that there was another London parkrun out there that had to be completed. This, coupled with the news that Hoblingwell would be starting soon after South Norwood, kind of made me think that maybe I couldn't win, that it was all a fruitless exercise. But that, ultimately, was the thought process of a man who just wanted to stop, who had felt he had done more than enough and deserved a rest. Luckily no more parkruns had started since then, and I therefore had plenty of time to run the 48th and 49th Greater London parkruns, though there was already a campaign in place for at least another one. But for now at least, I was about to become officially 'Lon-Done,' and could be satisfied that all boxes had finally been ticked.
Although it wasn't quite as cold as last week, I made sure to take some extra layers, and it was a good job I did, since I did feel cold on the journey home this week. I left the house at 7am and jogged down the road to the station to catch a Central Line train to Bond Street where I changed to the Jubilee Line to London Bridge to catch a train to Norwood Junction. The train was due to leave at 8.20am, and on looking at the board I had made the mistake of thinking that Norwood Junction was several stops along, and that I might actually get there too late. Luckily, soon after I realised it was actually the first stop, and needn't have panicked. The train pulled out and less than twenty minutes later I was stepping on to the platform

at Norwood Junction. I checked the map on my phone to determine which exit I needed from the station, and was soon jogging down Stanger Road to where it met Portland Road, looking for the side street that would take me more or less directly to South Norwood Country Park. I found a road and a grass path next to it, both going in the same direction past Croydon Sports Arena on the right, and soon came to the tram tracks where cars and pedestrians can cross at any time, providing they are looking both ways first. Not much further on was the visitor's centre where a small group had already gathered, so I stopped to use the loo and take off my tracksuit bottoms.

After confirming with the run director that it was best to leave my bag by the finish (further along the path) rather than the start, I jogged down the path, hoping I would have enough time to drop my bag and get back before the run began in not much more than ten minute's time. People were heading in the other direction, and I was keen to join them, so was relieved to find the finish wasn't as far away as I thought. I dropped my bag, wished the marshal there a good morning, then turned and headed back, reaching the start just as the briefing got underway.

A couple of runners arrived at the last moment, and the fairly large group assembled on the path. We had been warned by the run director that the path would be muddy and slippery, and that there may be some low branches, though neither of these things seemed to give anyone too many problems. We were soon off and running, heading down the path in the direction of the finish.


The Course

Especially compared to last week at Hoblingwell, this course is very straightforward. It is a two lap course running clockwise, beginning at the visitor's centre and finishing further down the path. It begins by heading north-east along the gently winding, wooded path, which can get a little muddy after wet weather, then opens up and passes the finish area, continuing on to the Elmer's End Road side of the park, past the lake, where it turns right along another wooded section, then right again at the corner. It then takes a left at a small group of trees and a marshal, then right and follows a long, straight section before turning right, then left along another straight towards the tram tracks where another marshal is stationed to direct you up a small hill to follow a track down to the small car park and beyond it the visitor's centre and the start of lap two. On reaching the visitor's centre/start a second time, there is just the short stretch onward to the finish line, which is just off the path on a stretch of grass.

Without as much warming up as I should have liked, I knew it wasn't going to be the best run, but I made sure not to start out too quickly like I had last week, and just try to keep a good pace all the way around. The course is fairly simple, but like most of the parks the scenery is enough to stop you from getting bored, and there are enough twists and turns to keep you focussed. Any park is better than a treadmill, and I'm sure in the summer Norwood Country Park is even better. I'd definitely come back.

Time: 23 minutes 38 seconds
Position: 24 out of 94

My only real aim this week was to beat my rather disappointing time at Hoblingwell the week before, which had almost been twenty-five minutes. I should have done more warming up, and I still hadn't quite adjusted to running in colder weather, but I definitely felt more prepared than last week, and made sure I didn't go too fast too soon. There were also less hills this week, only one very small one to speak of, and the terrain, while a little muddy in places, didn't cause any problems.

So what now? No doubt at some point in the near future I'll be writing up a report for number 50, and there may well, hopefully, be many more Greater London parkruns beyond that, but for now at least I'm (Lon) done with this particular challenge. I'm not done with parkrun tourism in general though, and intend to visit plenty more in the future including some abroad. What still remains to be the best part of parkrun tourism is the endless variety and surprise. Having a different course to do each time really helps to keep it interesting and challenging. That said, it is always good to run at my local, Gunnersbury Park, not only to try to better my time, but also because it means a lot less travel time and more sleep. Sleep . . . I remember that.

# Afterword

So, out of the many, many Greater London parkruns, which is my favourite? Trying to work that out would be a pointless waste of time. They're all fantastic for different reasons. I could choose Bushy because it's the original and the biggest, Burgess because I recorded my fastest ever 5k time there, Gunnersbury because it's my local parkrun and was my fiftieth parkrun overall, or Northala Fields because I ran it on my 40th birthday. But that's the thing – on paper there is no way of determining which is the best. It's all down to personal experience. If you want to know which of the Greater London parkruns is the best, you'll just have to get your running shoes on and get out there. Just remember to set your alarm clock for Saturday morning and not to forget your barcode!

Without wanting to try to boil the London parkruns down to a 'top ten,' I have instead decided to choose a few key categories, and list what would be my personal choices for each one based on my experiences completing this challenge.

And if you do decide to take on the 'Lon-done' challenge yourself, the very best of luck. It's quite a journey.

Dean Carter
April 2018

# Personal Parkrun Picks

### Most Picturesque

Ally Pally
Riddlesdown
Richmond Park

### Best Chance for a Personal Best time

Bushy Park
Burgess Park
Dulwich

### Friendliest/Most Sociable

Raphael
Bedfont Lakes
Southwark

### Best/Most Interesting Course (this is a tough one so I've chosen 5!)

Ally Pally
Bushy Park
Burgess Park
Peckham Rye
Lloyd

# Useful Greater London parkrun Information for Tourists

| Location | Nearest Train Stations | Toilets |
|---|---|---|
| Walthamstow | Highams Park (London Overground) | In the Peter May Sports Centre |
| Finsbury Park | Finsbury Park (National Rail, Piccadilly and Victoria Lines) or Manor House (Piccadilly Line) | By the café in the park |
| Ally Pally | Alexandra Palace (National Rail) or Wood Green (Piccadilly Line) | None as of 16/12/17 |
| Mile End | Mile End (Central, District and Hammersmith and City Lines) | Mile End stadium |
| Northala Fields | Northolt (Central Line) | At the San Remo Café |
| Tooting Common | Tooting Bec (Northern Line) | Tooting Bec running track |
| Southwark | Surrey Quays (London Overground), Bermondsey (Jubilee Line) | At the café |
| Bexley | Welling (National Rail), Bexleyheath (National Rail) | In the car park and at the boathouse |
| Barking | Barking (London Overground, National Rail, District Line, Hammersmith and City Line) | By the café |
| Fulham Palace | Putney Bridge (District Line) | |
| Riddlesdown | Whyteleafe (National Rail), Upper Warlingham (National Rail) | |

| | | |
|---|---|---|
| Old Deer Park | Richmond (National Rail, London Overground, District Line) | At Richmond Station and at Pools on the Park |
| Pymmes | Silver Street (London Overground) | Near the start of the run |
| Canons Park | Canons Park (Jubilee Line) | Disabled toilet near start |
| Valentines Park | Gants Hill (Central Line) | Near the Valentines Park Café and by the Gardener's Cottage Café. |
| Osterley | Osterley (Piccadilly Line) | Near the café. |
| Hilly Fields | Ladywell (National Rail) | At the back of the Pistachios Café block. |
| Harrow | Harrow-on-the-Hill (National Rail, Metropolitan Line) | Toilets in the St Mary's pavillion near the start, and a public toilet near the Hindes Road entrance. |
| Crystal Palace | Crystal Palace (London Overground, National Rail), Penge West (London Overground, National Rail) | Public toilets next to the start. |
| Beckenham Place Park | Ravensbourne (National Rail) | |
| Beckton | Royal Albert (DLR), Beckton Park (DLR) | |
| Richmond | Richmond (National Rail, London Overground, District Line) | |
| Crane Park | Whitton (South Western Railway) | |
| Wormwood Scrubs | East Acton (Central Line), White City (Central Line) | In the Linford Christie Sports Centre |
| Brockwell Park | Brixton (Southeastern), Herne Hill (Southeastern) | By the Brockwell Park Café |
| Dulwich | North Dulwich (National Rail) | By the Dulwich Clock Café |

| | | |
|---|---|---|
| Bedfont Lakes | Hatton Cross (Piccadilly Line) | |
| Hackney Marshes | Homerton (London Overground), Hackney Wick (London Overground) | In the Hackney Marshes Centre |
| Highbury Fields | Highbury and Islington (London Overground, Victoria Line) | Near the Highbury Pool and Fitness Centre |
| Hampstead Heath | Hampstead Heath (London Overground) | |
| Kingston | Kingston (National Rail) | |
| Oak Hill | Oakleigh Park Station (National Rail) | |
| Wanstead Flats | Leytonstone High Road (London Overground), Leytonstone (Central Line) | At the changing pavillion near the start. |
| Harrow Lodge | Elm Park (District Line) | At Hornchurch Sports Centre |
| Roundshaw Downs | East Croydon (National Rail) | |
| Orpington | Orpington (National Rail) | |
| Burgess Park | Elephant and Castle (Bakerloo Line, Northern Line) | At the tennis centre |
| Raphael Park | Gidea Park (TFL Rail) | At the café by the playground |
| Lloyd Park | East Croydon (National Rail) | |
| Gunnerbsury Park | South Ealing (Piccadilly line), Kew Bridge (National Rail) | |
| Bromley | Bromley South (National Rail) | At the pavillion near the finish line |
| Greenwich | Falconwood (National Rail) | |
| Peckham Rye | Honor Oak Park (London Overground, National Rail) | On Strakers Road |

| | | |
|---|---|---|
| Grovelands | Southgate (Piccadilly Line), Winchmore Hill (National Rail) | By the playground area. |
| Gladstone | Dollis Hill (Jubilee Line) | |
| Wimbledon Common | Wimbledon (District Line, National Rail) | |
| Bushy Park | Hampton Court (National Rail), Teddington (National Rail), Hampton Wick (National Rail) | Near play area |
| Hoblingwell | St. Mary Cray (National Rail) | In the clubhouse |
| South Norwood | Norwood Junction (National Rail, London Overground) | At the visitor's centre |

Printed in Great Britain
by Amazon